JAIME SALOM

BONFIRE AT DAWN

An historical tableau in four acts

based on the life and passion of

Fray Bartolomé de Las Casas

Translated by Phyllis Zatlin

ESTRENO
University Park, Pennsylvania
1992

ESTRENO Contemporary Spanish Plays 1
General Editor: Martha T. Halsey
Department of Spanish, Italian and Portuguese
College of the Liberal Arts
The Pennsylvania State University
University Park PA 16802 USA

Library of Congress Cataloging in Publication Data
Salom, Jaime, 1925-
Bonfire at Dawn

Bibligraphy:
Contents: Bonfire at dawn
1. Salom, Jaime, 1925-   Translation, English.
I. Zatlin, Phyllis. II. Title.
Library of Congress Catalog Card No.: 91-077384
ISBN: 0-9631212-0-0

Published with Support from

The Program of Cultural Cooperation Between
Spain's Ministry of Culture and the United States Universities
Office of Culture of the Spanish Embassy, Washington DC
The Pennsylvania State University

Cover: Jeffrey Eads

ESTRENO Collection of Contemporary Spanish Plays

General Editor: Martha T. Halsey

BONFIRE

AT

DAWN

NOT JUST A QUINCENTENNIAL PLAY

Forget Claudel, Fo, Ghelderode, and the others. Yes, they offer interesting perspectives on Christopher Columbus and his discovery, but Jaime Salom's *Bonfire at Dawn* is the play you've been seeking for 1992. Salom takes a searching look at the discovery's consequences, as witnessed by one who sailed in the third voyage of Columbus and participated in Spain's colonization of the New World. It is a true story, grippingly dramatized with clarity, impact, and economy of means.

Salom didn't have to fudge on historical events to achieve "political correctness." His meticulous research documented the terrible injustices inflicted upon native Americans in the name of Christianity, as well as the efforts of Bartolomé de Las Casas (1474-1566) to protect them. Salom's dramatization first depicts the great "Apostle of the Indians" as a poor but arrogant youth eager to see the lands his father had visited on the second voyage of Columbus. Las Casas later wrestles with his desire for power and with temptations of the flesh, including homosexuality. But he becomes a priest and faces still more daunting external obstacles.

Las Casas is a complex and flawed but compelling figure. The psychological drama of his developing conscience unfolds in counterpoint to the pageantry of the historical drama. As the action flows back and forth between Spain and America, the two opposing worlds are brought remarkably to life on a simple unit set, with a cast of only eleven men and four women. Salom's theatrical sensibilities extend to the play of sound and light, as when the exotic Indian flute music of young Las Casas's slave/companion returns to haunt him in his maturity. An illuminated antique map of the Americas doubles as a stained glass chapel window, and then spots of light appear on it to mark the places where Las Casas had left a legacy of hope rather than repression. At the death of Fray Bartolomé de Las Casas, the points of light become stars over his body.

Indeed, *Bonfire at Dawn* is not just a Columbus quincentennial play. It is a play for a new world at the dawn of a new era.

Felicia Hardison Londré
Dramaturg, Missouri Repertory Theatre

v

Jaime Salom

ABOUT THE PLAYWRIGHT

Jaime Salom was born in Barcelona in 1925. A practicing opthamologist, he began writing plays in the late 1940s, while completing his university training. He achieved his first Madrid production in 1960 and has since been one of Spain's most highly acclaimed and widely staged playwrights. His works have received numerous awards, including the National Literature Prize, various prizes of the Royal Spanish Academy, and recognition from El Espectador y la Crítica as best play of the year. Several of his plays have enjoyed record-breaking runs in Spain, have been performed successfully in other European countries and in Latin America, and have been made into films.

Salom's theatre is marked by its versatility. His major plays include *El baúl de los disfraces* (1964; The Trunk of Disguises), a poetic fantasy; *La casa de las chivas* (1968; Eng. trans. Barbara Carballal, "The House of the 'Chivas'"), a moralistic drama of the Spanish Civil War; *Los delfines* (1969; The Heirs Apparent), a political allegory anticipating the end of the Franco era; *Tiempo de espadas* (1972; Eng. trans. Marion P.Holt, "Time of Swords"), a political interpretation of The Last Supper; *La piel del limón* (1976; Eng. trans. Patricia W. O'Connor, *Bitter Lemon*), an impassioned plea for divorce reform; *El corto vuelo del gallo* (1980; Eng. trans. Marion P. Holt, *The Cock's Short Flight*), an expressionistic, historical drama focusing on Franco's libertarian father; and *Una hora sin television* (1987; An Hour Without Television), an intimate, two-character play, showing a marriage in crisis.

Although Salom has continually experimented with different theatrical modes, he has turned from time to time to Brechtian approaches to historical subjects. This dramatic current culminates in the Bartolomé de Las Casas text presented in this volume. *Una hoguera en el amanecer (Bonfire at Dawn)* was still running in Mexico, on tour, a year after the lavish production enjoyed a successful opening in the capital in late August 1990.

Una hoguera en el amanecer was first staged at the Jorge Negrete Theatre in Mexico City on 31 August 1991, under the direction of Sergio Olhovich.

The United States premiere of *Una hoguera en el amanecer* is scheduled for 30 January 1992 at the GALA Hispanic Theatre in Washington DC, under the direction of Hugo Medrano.

STAGE SET

Two levels. The upper one, stage right, has a ladder connecting it to the lower one, which takes up most of the stage.
The scenes are played on the two levels as indicated in the text.
The design should be a simple and suggestive outline.

COSTUMES

From the period, but modernized without being stereotyped.

CHARACTERS

Bartolomé de Las Casas
Fray Antonio de Montesinos
Gabriel
Fray Pedro de Córdoba
Pedro Las Casas
King Ferdinand - The Emperor (1)
Señor - Señor (Petrilla's son)
Pedro Rentería - Rodrigo de Andrada
The Governor
Bishop Fonseca - First Chancellor
Secretary Conchillos - Second Chancellor
Petrilla
María
Isabel (Mother)
Isabel (Daughter)

(1) The connecting dash identifies characters to be played by same actor.

ACT I

The deck of a ship. It is dawn on an April day in 1502. BARTOLOME is on deck, downstage, looking out at the sea. After a pause, his father, PEDRO LAS CASAS, enters. Sound of the sea and of seagulls.

PEDRO LAS CASAS: You're up early.

BARTOLOME: I didn't go to bed, Father. For two days now, dozens of seagulls have been hovering around our ships. I'm eager to see that New World.

PEDRO LAS CASAS: It's a difficult world, son. Very different from our neighborhood at San Lorenzo.

BARTOLOME: Since you returned from your first voyage, I've dreamed of this moment, of this land. Do you know what I find so attractive? Nothing will be impossible there.

PEDRO LAS CASAS: You're ambitious.

BARTOLOME: Everyday I give thanks to our Lord Admiral Columbus for restoring to us Spaniards our capacity to dream.

PEDRO LAS CASAS: You talk like a young boy, Bartolomé...not like a twenty-eight year-old man.

BARTOLOME: I still feel young, Father. And I hope to until I die. It's dawn already.

PEDRO LAS CASAS: This is the last time I'll be coming into this coast.

BARTOLOME: Only God can know that.

PEDRO LAS CASAS: I shall never return to our homeland. I want to bury my roots here forever.

BARTOLOME: What about Mother?

PEDRO LAS CASAS: At her age she doesn't need a man. She's used to my being away. I'll give our house to your sister as a dowry. When she marries, her husband can take care of both of them.

(*GABRIEL enters.*)

GABRIEL (*Trying to shake off his drowsiness, he takes deep breaths*): Beautiful morning.

PEDRO LAS CASAS: You're still half asleep, brother.

GABRIEL: Last night I finished off my last wineskin. It put me out, like a log. And if you only knew what's been going on in my head!

PEDRO LAS CASAS: Nightmares?

GABRIEL: Quite the opposite. I had my hands in jugs of gold. All of me glowed like hot coals from so much wealth. And all around me there were dozens of Indian girls with round breasts and sweaty thighs, offering themselves to me like tropical fruits.

PEDRO LAS CASAS (*Laughing*): Wake up!

GABRIEL: I emptied my bladder off the rail, so there's not a drop of wine left in my body. But I guarantee you that one day soon you're going to see me in the streets of Seville, loaded down with jewels and waited on by a flock of Indian maidens.

PEDRO LAS CASAS: You don't know what you're saying.

GABRIEL: I'm not going to be satisfied, like you on your other voyage with a few trinkets and a bag of gifts. I'm going to squeeze this land like an orange, to the last drop. I swear to God your brother's going to be a rich and powerful man, Pedro.

PEDRO LAS CASAS: Or a dead one.

GABRIEL: Maybe. But not a deadbeat or a nobody like the men in our family have always been.

(*A shot rings out.*)

BARTOLOME: Did you hear that? It's the cannon from the flagship. And now the others are answering.

(*PEDRO RENTERIA quickly scales the ladder. He is followed by PEDRO DE CORDOBA, an old Dominican friar.*)

PEDRO RENTERIA: You can see a strip of coast over there, where the sun is coming up.

VOICE: Land ho! To starboard! Land ho! Land ho!

(*Noises offstage of voices, shouts of happiness, shots fired from the long guns, music. The five men on stage hug each other in excitement.*)

PEDRO RENTERIA (*Kneeling*): Thank you, dear Lord.

(*PEDRO DE CORDOBA also kneels.*)

GABRIEL: Don't be impatient, girls. Gabriel's coming to love you all! And nobody better touch an ounce of my gold or one hair on my slaves' heads! (*With a cry of joy.*) Land!

BARTOLOME (*To Pedro*): Would you bless me, Father?

PEDRO LAS CASAS (*Putting his hand on his son's head*): May God always guide your steps. (*He gives his son a warm embrace.*) Bartolomé!

BARTOLOME: What about Mother? Aren't you thinking about her right now?

PEDRO LAS CASAS: This is not a land for a decent woman.

BARTOLOME: I can't stop thinking about her. About her and about our house in San Lorenzo...

(*On the lower level of the stage, ISABEL-MOTHER enters and sits down by the fire to mend a pile of clothes that she takes from a basket and shakes out.*)

PEDRO LAS CASAS: You'll have to learn to control your feelings.

BARTOLOME: I remember Christmas, four years ago, when you returned from your voyage...

(*Enter ISABEL-DAUGHTER.*)

ISABEL-DAUGHTER: Mother! The ships have arrived. The people are dancing for joy, cheering the sailors. Admiral Columbus has already come ashore...

ISABEL-MOTHER: May the Lord bless him.

BARTOLOME: Don't you sometimes remember that day?

PEDRO LAS CASAS: Sometimes.

ISABEL-MOTHER: Has your father arrived?

ISABEL-DAUGHTER: The men are just jumping off the ships. I came to see if you wanted to go down to the docks to greet him.

ISABEL-MOTHER: I said goodbye to him here when he left, and I'll wait for him here now that he's returned.

PEDRO LAS CASAS: But you have to get all that out of your system...if you're going to move ahead.

VOICES: Land ho! To starboard! Land ho! Land ho!

(*The action shifts to the lower level, to the house of the Las Casas family in 1498.*)

ISABEL-DAUGHTER: This will be the happiest Christmas of our lives.

ISABEL-MOTHER: I can't forget the ones we spent alone, saddened by his absence.

ISABEL-DAUGHTER: Aren't you happy about his return, Mother?

ISABEL-MOTHER: I've prayed for it every night. God had to hear me. But he won't stay with us long. I know him.

ISABEL-DAUGHTER: Father went to get us out of poverty.

ISABEL-MOTHER: We've always been poor. We're used to it. But when Admiral Columbus came to Seville the first time and we went, like everybody else, to look at his grand entourage, your father became so intoxicated that he cursed his misfortune and stopped accepting God's will.

ISABEL-DAUGHTER: It was God who allowed them to discover a new world!

ISABEL-MOTHER: One that will only bring us troubles and sorrow.

ISABEL-DAUGHTER: And gold.

ISABEL-MOTHER: Yes. Also gold, and silver, and precious stones...but only for the rich, Isabel, the way it happens in every war. Because this is nothing but a war, another one, although this time the enemies are just poor unfortunates who are neither evil nor hypocritical.

ISABEL-DAUGHTER: But they're going to teach them religion so that they will go to Heaven!

ISABEL-MOTHER: God grant that we not bury them in hell.

ISABEL-DAUGHTER: Why do you always see the bad in everything? Oh, Mother, I'm so happy, so happy!

(*PEDRO LAS CASAS and BARTOLOME have come down the steps from the upper level of the stage.*)

PEDRO LAS CASAS: Hello there! Is there a room for a tired Spaniard who's crossed the sea?

ISABEL-DAUGHTER: Father!

PEDRO LAS CASAS (*Hugging her*): My little lark. I found our Latin student at the foot of the ship's ladder.

BARTOLOME: Master Nebrija cancelled classes so we could welcome you.

PEDRO LAS CASAS (*To Isabel-Mother*): And you, Señora Isabel, won't you open the sweet harbor of your arms to me?

ISABEL-MOTHER (*Getting up*): Pedro...

PEDRO LAS CASAS: Isabel, Isabel...I hope your fears have finally vanished. Here we are again, together and happy, ready to celebrate Christmas.

ISABEL-DAUGHTER: Did you come back rich?

PEDRO LAS CASAS: No.

BARTOLOME: But you've seen fascinating places and had the most extraordinary adventures.

PEDRO LAS CASAS: Yes, in that sense, I'm certainly rich. I've done more living in these few years than other people in a lifetime.

BARTOLOME: They say that there are thousands of rivers and trees with leaves bigger than a man, and bird feathers so dazzling they would blind you.

PEDRO LAS CASAS: Oh, Bartolomé, you're exaggerating again. There are beautiful landscapes, but hardly anybody bothers to admire them, and the horizons glisten, but there's no time to look that far. One's eyes are turned downward, to the earth, wondering how much gold is in its bowels and whether or not the natives will be strong enough to bring it out before they drop dead from fatigue.

ISABEL-MOTHER: Her Highness the Queen will not permit that.

PEDRO LAS CASAS: The Queen cannot see everything. And the only creed respected there is one's own greed. But there will be plenty of time to astound you with all the things I have to tell you. I've brought you presents, lots of presents.

ISABEL-DAUGHTER: Oh, good!
PEDRO LAS CASAS (*Clapping*): Come in. (*An INDIAN boy appears, carrying a bundle.*)
INDIAN: Señor... (*He kneels at Pedro's feet.*)
PEDRO LAS CASAS: This is Lorenzo. I baptized him with the name of our parish saint. But we call him Señor because that's the only word he's learned in our language. (*To the Indian boy.*) Isn't that so?
SEÑOR (*Nodding and smiling*): Señor, señor.
ISABEL-MOTHER: He's just a boy. (*She holds out her arms to give him a hug*). Come, child.
SEÑOR (*Frightened, he hides behind Pedro Las Casas*): Señor, Señor!
ISABEL-DAUGHTER: Silly, she's not going to do anything to you. (*She and BARTOLOME laugh. ISABEL-DAUGHTER goes over to Señor and caresses him.*) My mother only wanted to welcome you to our house. (*She takes him over to her mother, who kisses him.*) You see? Like another son.
ISABEL-MOTHER: How sad and frightened his eyes are.
PEDRO LAS CASAS: Characteristic of his race. Just like the color of his skin. Some say they're just a species of animal created to serve man.
ISABEL-MADRE: How can they say such a blasphemous thing?
PEDRO LAS CASAS: I don't believe it, of course, even though he can't speak a Christian language.
BARTOLOME: I'll teach him, Father.
PEDRO LAS CASAS: He's very intelligent. Let me show you. (*Calling him.*) Boy.
SEÑOR (*Moving away from the mother*): Señor.
PEDRO LAS CASAS (*Gesturing a great deal so that Señor will understand*): Bring the bundle here and untie it. (*They all laugh at how quickly Señor obeys.*)
ISABEL-DAUGHTER: What did you bring us?
PEDRO LAS CASAS: Incredible surprises. (*He picks up a bag*). Pearls of all sizes and tones, snatched from the rocks of the river banks, so your mother can shine like a princess.
ISABEL-MOTHER: The only adornment I've ever wanted was honesty.
PEDRO LAS CASAS: There's no connection.
ISABEL-DAUGHTER: They're gorgeous.
PEDRO LAS CASAS: For you, my little lark, these stones for jewelry sets and earrings.
ISABEL-DAUGHTER: Oh, Father!
PEDRO LAS CASAS: Fabrics and blankets woven by the natives in their huts. Seeds you've never seen before that give off intoxicating perfumes when you split them open.
BARTOLOME: And what's this?
PEDRO LAS CASAS: Charms, to keep them from harm, in battle or in sickness, in childbirth or during the hunt.

ISABEL-MOTHER: That's witchcraft.
PEDRO LAS CASAS: They're just curiosities; don't be frightened.

(*Suddenly the INDIAN boy takes one of the charms in his hands. He is obviously very moved and clearly indicates that he wants it for himself.*)

SEÑOR: Señor, Señor!
PEDRO LAS CASAS: What is it? Give it to me. I said to give it to me. Right now! (*The INDIAN boy resists and PEDRO threatens to hit him.*) Damn Indian!
BARTOLOME: No!
PEDRO LAS CASAS: I know how to treat him. (*The frightened boy gives it to him and Pedro strokes his hair as if he were a little animal.*) That's it. Good Indian. It's a charm from his tribe.
ISABEL-MOTHER: Are you giving it to me as a present?
PEDRO LAS CASAS: It's for you, my dear.
ISABEL-MOTHER (*Taking it and handing it to the boy*): Here, child.

(*The INDIAN is afraid he will be punished if he accepts it. Then, seeing that no one is threatening him, he gradually approaches.*)

PEDRO LAS CASAS: You can accept it. Your mistress is offering it to you.
SEÑOR (*He takes it and puts it around his neck then kneels in front of Isabel-Mother*): Señor.
ISABEL-MOTHER (*Lifting him up from the floor*): You poor little boy.
BARTOLOME: Father, you've brought presents for everyone but me. Are you dissatisfied with my conduct?
PEDRO LAS CASAS: Quite the contrary. I know how well you've applied yourself to the study of Latin. I'm proud of my son.
BARTOLOME: Then...
PEDRO LAS CASAS: That's why I've brought you the best present, the only one that can go with you throughout the city and sooth your ears with the sound of his flute. (*He hands the Indian boy over.*) He's yours.
BARTOLOME: Mine?
PEDRO LAS CASAS: Treat him with tolerance but use his services as you please.
BARTOLOME: You mean that I'm going to have a page, as if I were a gentleman?
PEDRO LAS CASAS (*To the Indian boy*): This is Bartolomé your new master.
SEÑOR: Señor... (He starts to kneel but BARTOLOME takes him by the hands).
BARTOLOME: Bartolomé, Bartolomé.
SEÑOR: Señor...Bartolóme.
BARTOLOME: That's it. Bartolóme.

SEÑOR (*Suddenly all smiles*): Bartolóme, señor, señor Bartolóme. (*Very happy, he takes his reed flute from his belt and, dancing contentedly, he begins to play some joyously sweet notes that repeat these words with their melody.*)

BARTOLOME: That's it. Bartolóme, Bartolóme. And that's Isabel, and that's Mother, and that's Father.

SEÑOR: Bartolóme señor, señor Bartolóme.

ISABEL-MOTHER: Set the table, daughter. And this time, praise be to God, put out two more bowls.

PEDRO LAS CASAS: Lorenzo will eat alone.

ISABEL-MOTHER: In my parents' house, we all ate at the same table, masters and servants.

PEDRO LAS CASAS: Woman, he wouldn't feel comfortable. He eats in any old corner. It's his custom.

ISABEL-MOTHER: Not mine.

PEDRO LAS CASAS: Besides, he isn't a servant. I bought him.

ISABEL-MOTHER: From whom?

PEDRO LAS CASAS: From his owner. A merchant.

ISABEL-MOTHER: Under my roof, Pedro Las Casas, nobody is the property of anybody.

PEDRO LAS CASAS: Even the bishops and the abbots have slaves.

ISABEL-MOTHER: You're not a bishop or an abbot that I know of.

BARTOLOME: But, Mother...

ISABEL-MOTHER: And you aren't either, son.

PEDRO LAS CASAS: But he's so proud and happy with his new master! Aren't you, Señor?

ISABEL-MOTHER: Not in my house.

PEDRO LAS CASAS: That's enough. I'm back and this house has a master again. (*To Isabel-Daughter.*) You, set the table like your mother told you. (*To Isabel-Mother.*) You put away the things I brought in the bedroom chest. (*The two women exit.*) And you, son, go with Señor to the tavern and buy two jugs of their best wine so you and I can celebrate my return like men. (*He gives him a coin.*) What can women know of the work, the dangers, the harshness of life over there...where every morning one wonders if he'll make it to nightfall, if he will have the strength to bear such exhaustion?

(*FRAY ANTONIO, in his Dominican habit, appears next to them. He kneels on a prayer bench and begins to pray.*)

BARTOLOME: Father, I'm very glad you've returned.

PEDRO LAS CASAS: Someday you'll go with me and you'll experience the anguish for yourself.

BARTOLOME: I would like that.

PEDRO LAS CASAS: Go along now, and don't dally. I'm really thirsty.

(BARTOLOME and the INDIAN BOY exit. PEDRO watches them leave. Then he follows them. We hear bells ringing. PEDRO DE CORDOBA slowly descends from the upper stage and crosses to his companion.)

PEDRO DE CORDOBA: I'm sorry to disturb your prayers, Fray Antonio.

FRAY ANTONIO: I was just meditating on the second Vesper psalm.

PEDRO DE CORDOBA: The Father General has ordered me to come here to the Convent of San Gabriel on a mission that must not be unknown to you.

FRAY ANTONIO: What can the Father General be seeking in this isolated corner of Extremadura?

PEDRO DE CORDOBA: He has asked me to select a small group of friars to help me at the convent on the island of Hispaniola, and I thought of you. *(Pause.)* Well, what is your opinion?

FRAY ANTONIO: Obedience is the first rule of a Dominican.

PEDRO DE CORDOBA: Then I order you to open your heart to me, in all sincerity.

FRAY ANTONIO: I entered the religious life with the sole wish of praying and meditating within the walls of this cell, even to be buried within the cloister until God shall call me to judgment.

PEDRO DE CORDOBA: But do you feel no desire to attract to the Lord the flocks of heretics and pagans who will otherwise fall into eternal damnation?

FRAY ANTONIO: It is my greatest desire, Fray Pedro. I pray for them constantly. I fast and I practice self-mortification.

PEDRO DE CORDOBA: But you belong to a preaching order.

FRAY ANTONIO: And you know very well that my poor sermons lack the necessary eloquence and rhetoric. I am shy, and when I preach, in my mind I confuse phrases and concepts.

PEDRO DE CORDOBA: Are you afraid of death? Of violence, of treachery, of ingratitude?

FRAY ANTONIO: I am afraid, Fray Pedro, that I have all of the defects of a common man who has taken refuge in the Order to conceal his weaknesses.

PEDRO DE CORDOBA: And are you not tempted to take our truth to infidel lands, with a martyr's heroism if necessary?

FRAY ANTONIO: I do not consider myself worthy of such an honor.

PEDRO DE CORDOBA: Have you been sincere with me, Fray Antonio?

FRAY ANTONIO: As if you had heard me in confession. I am sorry to have disappointed you.

PEDRO DE CORDOBA: By this very night, have your baggage ready. The order to leave may come at any moment.

FRAY ANTONIO: I fail to understand.

PEDRO DE CORDOBA: I do not want adventurers, or heroes, or mystics. But men capable of feeling anguish as our Lord anguished on His last night. What was the subject of your meditation?
FRAY ANTONIO: The Annunciation to Our Lady.
PEDRO DE CORDOBA: "Behold I am the handmaid of the Lord; let it be to me according to your word." I ask you to forgive me for taking you away from the peace of your convent...and to pray for this poor friar. Do you feel overwhelmed?
FRAY ANTONIO: Very much so.
PEDRO DE CORDOBA: Just between you and me, Fray Antonio Montesinos, I do, too. (*FRAY ANTONIO goes back to his prayers. PEDRO DE CORDOBA stops before exiting by the stairs that lead to the upper stage.*) By the way, do you get seasick?
FRAY ANTONIO: I do not know. I've never been on a ship or even seen the sea.

(*PETRILLA enters the lower stage, singing and dancing seguidillas or other Andalusian music from the period. A short time later GABRIEL comes down from the upper stage. It is night.*)

PETRILLA (*Singing*): The evening time in Seville, Seville,
        Jasmin scent on the dew,
        Fills me with the aromas of life,
        Fills me with thoughts of you.
        Fragrance, love and joy in the garden,
        Beside the deep river,
        Lovely songs waft to me on the breeze
        Of the Guadalquivir.

GABRIEL: Give me a jug of Petrilla wine, you who are the most fragrant and beautiful flower along this shore.
PETRILLA: And you are the most talkative trickster I've met since I've been in the city.
GABRIEL: I shall become forever mute, like a little owl, for just one kiss from your lips.
PETRILLA: Be careful. I may take you at your word.
GABRIEL (*Puckering up*): I'm ready.
PETRILLA (*Laughing*): Shall I bring you some slices of ham?
GABRIEL: To tempt my mouth I've already got your hocks...there's no little pig in the world as appetizing or as well displayed.
PETRILLA: Don Gabriel, you're making me angry.
GABRIEL: Don, what's this "Don" business? You call my nephew just Bartolomé.
PETRILLA: That's different.
GABRIEL: Because he's younger or because you're in love with him?

PETRILLA: What I feel in my heart, I don't go about saying to everyone.
GABRIEL: But your eyes do, silly.
PETRILLA: You think you're clever.
GABRIEL: He's buried in his Latin and someday he'll be a priest. He's not husband material.
PETRILLA: What does that matter to me!
GABRIEL: I, on the other hand, am a widower.
PETRILLA: As if you'd marry me. What a joker.
GABRIEL: Why not? In the whole world there wouldn't be a bride more luscious and beautiful than you.
PETRILLA: Nor such an old, hang-down bridegroom.
GABRIEL: You've got a sharp tongue.
PETRILLA: From answering men's lies.
GABRIEL: Don't you believe me?
PETRILLA: I believed that old line once, when I was still a little girl. He was a water carrier, very strong, who came to town for the fair. I could see myself going through God's world calling out "Water, water." And as you see, now I sell wine.
GABRIEL: And if I were to tell you that someday I will take off across the sea and be owner of an island like Admiral Columbus and send for you to cover you with jewels?
PETRILLA: I would answer that you're quite a faker.
GABRIEL: Leave your bedroom window open when you get through work at the tavern and we'll continue this chat.
PETRILLA: What do you think I am?
GABRIEL: More than once I've seen my nephew clamber up the grapevine and his little Indian page asleep down below, leaning on the trunk and waiting until dawn for his master.
PETRILLA: You must have been drunk.
GABRIEL: Or jealous, Petrilla. (*He kisses her. She lets him but then pulls away.*) Tonight I'm going to wait under the arbor, eating grapes.
PETRILLA (*Laughing*): They're green.
GABRIEL: I'll wait until they ripen.
PETRILLA (*She laughs. Then she resumes her dance, flirting with Gabriel*):
        The evening time in Seville, Seville,
        Jasmin scent on the dew,
        Fills me with the aromas of life,
        Fills me with thoughts of you.

(*BARTOLOME has entered.*)

BARTOLOME: Petrilla...have you seen Señor?
GABRIEL: Bring another jug for my nephew.
BARTOLOME: Hello, Uncle Gabriel. (*To Petrilla.*) I've been looking for him all evening. The constables have come to take him and send him

back to his homeland. You know the Queen has issued a decree abolishing slavery for all of her vassals on both sides of the ocean.

PETRILLA: Hurray for the Queen. Men should not be the masters of women nor should white people be the masters of blacks.

GABRIEL: Forget that philosophy stuff and get me more wine.

BARTOLOME: He's been sulking and downcast since the news came.

PETRILLA (*Returning with two jugs. She serves one to Gabriel and approaches Bartolomé with the other*): May I drink from your mug?

BARTOLOME: Why not?

PETRILLA: You shall know my secret. Although all Seville already knows who is the owner of my heart.

BARTOLOME: There must be more than one.

PETRILLA: Don't be cruel. I swear to you that there is no one like you. Not now or ever!

GABRIEL: To your health, nephew, and to that of this charming creature.

PETRILLA: Thank you.

BARTOLOME: To your health, uncle. (*He drinks.*) I thought since you and Señor are such good friends and you always stand up for him, perhaps you know where I can find him.

PETRILLA: Maybe. Don't you find me attractive anymore?

BARTOLOME: I'm not made of stone.

PETRILLA: Well then.

BARTOLOME: But that body could be my downfall.

PETRILLA: Or your good fortune. Go to the riverbank. Sometimes he's down there, immersed in thought and watching the current for hours. (*BARTOLOME starts to exit.*) Will you be coming back?

BARTOLOME: No.

GABRIEL: You heard him. He's not coming back. And the night will be much too long and fragrant to sleep alone.

PETRILLA: You are a hopeless rogue and scoundrel.

GABRIEL: And a widower who'll someday be rich!

PETRILLA: That I'll have to see. (*He takes her by the waist, and they both disappear, laughing.*)

BARTOLOME: Señor...Lorenzo...Señor! (*Suddenly he discovers SEÑOR over to one side. He is squatting, motionless. He stares at the river and plays his flute.*) What are you doing here? (*SEÑOR continues playing.*) I've been looking for you for hours. So now tell me, what's wrong.

SEÑOR: Señor Bartolóme knows.

BARTOLOME: Don't be a child. You no longer have an owner. You're free. You will return to your land and be with your people.

SEÑOR: Father died. Mother died. No more tribe. Only Arawak medal. (*He points to the charm that he wears hanging from his neck.*) Here.

BARTOLOME: But that is your country, your people. Someday you will find a beautiful girl and have a Christian family. You'll have many children.

SEÑOR: I no have children. I no girl. I no country. I, Señor Bartolóme, my whole life.

BARTOLOME: That's not possible, Señor.

SEÑOR: I ask Señor Queen Isabella stay Seville.

BARTOLOME: You'd have to have legal papers, contracts, a royal order.

SEÑOR: I stay! I stay!

BARTOLOME: We'll try, I promise you. But for now you have to go.

SEÑOR: I go with Señor Bartolóme. I wait under Petrilla's window. I carry books. I shave you. I sleep foot of bed.

BARTOLOME: I couldn't pay you. I'm poor.

SEÑOR: I no money. Family Señor Bartolóme my family. Children Señor Bartolóme my children.

BARTOLOME: I'm not going to have a family or children, Señor. Some day I'll be a priest. Although at times... I'm from Seville. I have hot blood, and the air smells of jazmin. In spite of myself, once in a while I fall in love. But you wouldn't understand.

SEÑOR: Señor understand Señor Bartolóme. Señor smell jazmin. Señor in love.

BARTOLOME: You? Well yes, of course.

SEÑOR: Señor love. Señor great love.

BARTOLOME (*Laughing*): So tell me, who is it that you love, Señor?

SEÑOR: No!

BARTOLOME: Let me guess. Petrilla? (*SEÑOR shakes his head no.*) My sister Isabel? (*Vigorous shaking of head as if the suggestion were sacrilegious.*) Well then, I command you. Tell me. Who?

SEÑOR (*Crying*): No, no, no!

BARTOLOME: You're still my slave and you have to obey me.

SEÑOR (*Following a long pause*): Señor Bartolóme. (*He covers his face in embarrassment.*)

BARTOLOME (*Laughing*): That's not the kind of love I meant.

SEÑOR: No other love.

BARTOLOME: But there are God's laws, nature's laws.

SEÑOR (*Firmly*): And Love.

BARTOLOME (*Becoming aware of Señor's true feelings*): That's enough!

SEÑOR: Señor Bartolóme love Señor?

BARTOLOME: Of course I love you, but...

SEÑOR: I your slave. I yours, all yours!

BARTOLOME: Dear God, your way of confusing things horrifies me.

SEÑOR: Señor no confuse. (*He takes Bartolomé's hand and kisses it tenderly.*)

BARTOLOME (*Gently pulling his hand away*): Leave me alone, Señor. Go home. No! Wait. Sometimes boys feel a great admiration for someone my age. They see him as a model and want to be like him, become one with him. It happened to me with my father. I wanted to imitate him and be a merchant. For a smile from him or a word of praise I would have given my life. But that's very different from what you're suggesting.

SEÑOR: Señor Bartolóme confuse.

BARTOLOME: Later on, when you're grown up and happy with a Christian wife who loves and respects you, you'll understand your confusion now.

SEÑOR: Señor obey. Señor have wife, be happy. But Señor love only Señor Bartolóme.

BARTOLOME: Listen.

SEÑOR (*Clinging to him, crying*): Señor Bartolóme confuse. Confuse!

BARTOLOME (*Aware of the truth, draws away*): Tomorrow morning they'll come to take you. You will set sail on the next ship and they'll take you to your land and we'll never see each other again.

SEÑOR: No!

BARTOLOME: It's for the best.

SEÑOR: Señor ask favor Señor Bartolóme. Favor, favor. Yes?

BARTOLOME: What is it?

SEÑOR (*Taking the medal from his neck and giving it to Bartolomé*): Wear always?

BARTOLOME: I will. (*SEÑOR exits rapidly, crying. BARTOLOME is left holding the medal. He puts it on. Then he calls out in anguish.*) Señor!

(*Lights up on the deck of the ship where PEDRO LAS CASAS, GABRIEL, PEDRO DE CORDOBA, and PEDRO RENTERIA are standing. BARTOLOME goes up the stairs to join them. Sound of a gun shot.*)

GABRIEL: Did you hear? It's the cannon on the flagship.

(*More shots.*)

PEDRO LAS CASAS: And now the others are answering.

PEDRO RENTERIA: You can see a strip of coast over there, where the sun is coming up.

VOICE: Land ho! To starboard! Land ho! Land ho!

(*Sound of voices, shouts of happiness, shots fired from the long guns.*)

PEDRO RENTERIA (*Kneeling*): Thank you, dear Lord.

(*PEDRO DE CORDOBA also kneels.*)

PEDRO LAS CASAS (*Putting his hand on Bartolomé's head*): You spent the night on the deck, like a knight standing watch over his arms. May this land give to you the honor and glory that you seek.

BARTOLOME: Amen. (*Father and son embrace.*)

PEDRO LAS CASAS: I'm only a merchant, my son. I came on the other trip with Admiral Columbus to be with my little cargo of goods. But you are a learned man and a teacher of Church doctrine. I am sure that you will earn respect from one coast to the other for our family name, our heritage as converted Jews.

BARTOLOME: I bring the treasure of a Doctrine that I shall explain like a big brother to his little brothers.

PEDRO LAS CASAS: Although I am but an ignorant man, let me give you one piece of advice. Never take advantage of that Doctrine for your personal benefit.

BARTOLOME: But, Father...

PEDRO LAS CASAS: Our faith is so true and so powerful that many bandy it about here to defend their causes, good and bad. My father gave me a similar piece of advice when I began my work: Never invoke the Lord's name to sell damaged merchandise.

BARTOLOME: I shall not forget.

GABRIEL (*Approaching the others*): The sea is covered with canoes of natives coming to meet us.

PEDRO LAS CASAS: They've raised the banner of the Virgin Mary on the captain's ship.

PEDRO RENTERIA (*Waving*): Here comes a boat with some Spaniards. Ahoy there! God be with you!

DISTANT VOICES: Gold, lots of gold. And an uprising of the natives in the north!

GABRIEL: Did you hear? Gold and a chance to take captives in a war. We're in luck!

PEDRO LAS CASAS: Look. A man has jumped off one of the canoes and is swimming this way.

BARTOLOME: He'll drown. He's crazy.

GABRIEL: They're like little animals--not the least bit rational.

BARTOLOME: No, no, it can't be.

PEDRO LAS CASAS: Just then I thought so, too.

BARTOLOME: It is. I saw him raise his face to breathe.

GABRIEL (*Laughing*): Now they're lifting him on a rope, as if he were a fish they were going to fry.

BARTOLOME (*Calling*): Señor! Señor!

PEDRO LAS CASAS: It is he.

(*SEÑOR climbs the stairs, dripping wet.*)

SEÑOR: Señor Bartolóme! Señor Bartolóme! (*He throws himself at Bartolomé's feet. BARTOLOME lifts him up.*)

BARTOLOME: My dear friend. You're so thin!

SEÑOR: I'm so happy, Señor Bartolóme, to see you at last!

BARTOLOME: But how did you find me?

SEÑOR: I knew ships going to arrive. I knew Señor Bartolóme come to my land. I escape from the mine. I leave everything and come running. Three days without sleep.

PEDRO LAS CASAS: But they will punish you.

SEÑOR: It doesn't matter. I'm happy. Señor is happy.

GABRIEL: He's an escapee. The laws are very strict. We must inform the authorities.

BARTOLOME: Be still.

GABRIEL: It's my obligation to report this.

BARTOLOME: Don't move. Or I'll kill you. I swear that if you report him I'll kill you.

GABRIEL: You idiot. We have to hand him over or they'll hang us all.

END OF FIRST ACT

ACT II

On the island of Hispaniola, 1509. La Concepción, Bartolomé's estate. FRAY ANTONIO MONTESINOS is standing with his back to us. BARTOLOME enters. He is wearing a colonist's straw hat and carries a riding whip in his hand.

FRAY ANTONIO: Bartolomé de las Casas?

BARTOLOME: With whom do I have the honor...?

FRAY ANTONIO: A humble friar from the port of Santo Domingo.

BARTOLOME: It's a long way and the sun is hot. You'll have some fresh coconut milk with me.

FRAY ANTONIO: Thank you.

BARTOLOME (*He offers it to him and they both drink*): It's as refreshing as melted snow.

FRAY ANTONIO: Indeed.

BARTOLOME: Then, if you like, I'll show you the plantation. With the help of the Indians that Admiral Columbus assigned to me, I hope to turn it into the most fertile one in the area. I shall send you a case of fruit to try.

FRAY ANTONIO: Thank you.

BARTOLOME: I suppose that you've come to request a donation for your convent. Although I tithe faithfully to the church, no one ever leaves here without a few coins. (*He looks in his wallet.*)

FRAY ANTONIO: I come not in search of your money but of your heart.

BARTOLOME: Around here my heart is generally of less interest than my purse.

FRAY ANTONIO: On one of my trips to the interior I met an old friend of yours.

BARTOLOME: A Spaniard?

FRAY ANTONIO: A native. He had been handed over to a compatriot of ours who, like so many others, is getting rich from a gold mine at the expense of the Indians' health.

BARTOLOME: Is the boy's name Señor?

FRAY ANTONIO: He gave me a different name, Lorenzo. And he is not a boy but a sick old man, lying in a hut on a hammock.

BARTOLOME: My God!

FRAY ANTONIO: Ever since he was cruelly punished for leaving his work... Years ago, when you arrived on the island. He wants to see you before he dies. It seems that this desire alone has kept him alive, in spite of the prognosis. Here is a map of the route; it is only two days away.

BARTOLOME: We're just in the middle of harvesting the sugar cane.

FRAY ANTONIO: You cannot wait if you want to see him alive.

BARTOLOME: From what you say, he has been sick a long time.

FRAY ANTONIO: Not like now. Will you go?

BARTOLOME: Yes.

FRAY ANTONIO: May God bless you.

BARTOLOME (*Going upstage. PEDRO LAS CASAS appears*): Father! Have my horse saddled. I shall be away several days.

PEDRO LAS CASAS: You can't leave the plantation. The crop is ripe and it could be lost because of the heat.

BARTOLOME: You can take charge.

PEDRO LAS CASAS: They won't obey me. You know them. They'll lie down in the shade and do nothing.

BARTOLOME: So give them watermelon to refresh them.

PEDRO LAS CASAS: Have you lost your mind? What will your uncle Gabriel say? He's getting married tomorrow.

BARTOLOME: Have them cut all of the flowers on the plantation to decorate the chapel. And with the white ones, make a bouquet for Petrilla. Please, Father, I'm in a hurry.

(*PEDRO LAS CASAS exits in a state of upset.*)

FRAY ANTONIO: May God see that you arrive in time.

BARTOLOME: It's outrageous. We try to make Christians of them and they treat them like dogs.

FRAY ANTONIO: That's true.

BARTOLOME: Here we teach them doctrine, we take them to Sunday mass, and we give them their rations of meat.

FRAY ANTONIO: But they work day and night for you.

BARTOLOME: For the plantation. We all work.

FRAY ANTONIO: But this is their land...and now it is yours.

BARTOLOME: The King gave it to me.

FRAY ANTONIO: Our King.

BARTOLOME: By order of the Pope.

FRAY ANTONIO: Our Pope.

BARTOLOME: I don't like your line of reasoning. Please tell me your name.

FRAY ANTONIO: A humble Dominican.

BARTOLOME: But you must have a name.

FRAY ANTONIO: Antonio. Fray Antonio Montesinos.

BARTOLOME: I shall not forget.

(*BARTOLOME exits. We hear the neighing of his horse and the pounding of the hoofs. The sound of gregorian chants is superimposed. Enter several Dominican friars, following a cross, on their way to the chapel. We only recognize PEDRO DE CORDOBA and FRAY ANTONIO DE MONTESINOS. They stop. All of them surround Pedro de Córdoba and kneel. He blesses them.*)

PEDRO DE CORDOBA: May the Lord grant to us a holy and recuperative sleep.

ALL: Amen. (*They begin to withdraw. BARTOLOME has appeared to one side.*)

BARTOLOME: Fray Antonio.

FRAY ANTONIO: You're here?

BARTOLOME: I need to speak to your heart, just as a few days ago you came to speak to mine.

FRAY ANTONIO: Speak.

BARTOLOME: The Indian boy has died.

FRAY ANTONIO: At last God has granted him the rest that he was denied on earth. Did you have the consolation of seeing him before he died?

BARTOLOME: Indeed I ran my mare into the ground. But he had breathed his last some hours before. I only saw his tattered body, an old rigid body, as if of wood, that they covered with dirt and were not even going to put a cross.

FRAY ANTONIO: Unfortunately the scene is a familiar one.

BARTOLOME: I feel sick, very sick. And there is no one who can understand my sorrow like you.

FRAY ANTONIO: Why did you not seek him before, considering that you held him in such esteem?

BARTOLOME: I did not wish to keep him at my side...for personal reasons. May I speak to you in confession?

FRAY ANTONIO: From this moment on, all that you say will be held secret.

BARTOLOME: He had a special--inclination--towards me. That is why I thought a total separation would be best.

FRAY ANTONIO: Best for him, or also for you?

BARTOLOME: I don't understand.

FRAY ANTONIO: No one is master of his own feelings.

BARTOLOME: Since he went away, I have thought of him often. Perhaps too often. But that was something I thought I had already erased from my mind. Until I saw his dead body and everything came back more forcefully than ever.

FRAY ANTONIO: You obeyed God's law.

BARTOLOME: But he is dead. He died little by little since they--since I-- sent him to the mines. (*We hear the music of the flute.*) If you could have known him when he came to Seville! He was the liveliest and most animated boy imaginable. And the day I arrived at the island, he risked his life to see me for a few moments. While I did nothing to save him.

FRAY ANTONIO: You avoided temptation.

BARTOLOME: At first I tried to numb myself with carnal pleasures --God forgive me. Then I imposed a harsh chastity and abstinence, without respite. Now I ask myself if that was virtue, or a sinful fidelity that is a thousand times more guilty.

FRAY ANTONIO: You must calm yourself.

BARTOLOME: I am known for treating my Indians more gently than any other Spaniard. But perhaps I do so because they are Señor's brothers and they share the color of his skin. In that case I am worse than anyone else, because I do it for unnatural motives. I am not defending them. I am defending Señor.

FRAY ANTONIO: Those are the devil's thoughts.

BARTOLOME: Although sometimes I hate them and I want to treat them with cruelty--because none of them is Señor. (*Pause. The flute music ends.*)

FRAY ANTONIO: His dead body has affected you. I can remember hundreds, no thousands of them. Just as old, just as rigid, without even a cross to remember their soul. It makes me sick inside to think that we want to sell them our faith at the price of drawing from them the last drop of their lives.

BARTOLOME: Many treat them with charity.

FRAY ANTONIO: That's not enough.

BARTOLOME: Charity is one of the three great virtues.

FRAY ANTONIO: Not when justice is scorned! It is a virtue to bury those we have killed from exhaustion, to help deliver the baby of the woman we have raped, to give a handful of corn to those whose wealth we have stolen. But it is unjust!

BARTOLOME: Be careful of what you say.

FRAY ANTONIO: Good Lord! Don't you see that in the name of God we are crucifying a people? Even if some of us are so virtuous that we hold up to their lips a sponge soaked in vinegar and gall.

BARTOLOME: Unfortunately they are not angels from Paradise, as Admiral Columbus at first believed. And we must lead them away from their horrible customs.

FRAY ANTONIO: While respecting their gold, their land, their women and their leaders.

BARTOLOME: Now you are the one who must calm yourself.

FRAY ANTONIO: You must excuse me. It is not easy for me either that no one understands me. Perhaps from now on you will. (*Long pause.*)

BARTOLOME: Before you go, I ask that you absolve me for what I told you. (*He kneels.*)

FRAY ANTONIO: Your plantation chapelain can forgive your sins.

BARTOLOME: I don't understand.

FRAY ANTONIO: I cannot.

BARTOLOME (*Getting up*): You refuse?

FRAY ANTONIO: I would be committing a great sacrilege.

BARTOLOME: You're insulting me.

FRAY ANTONIO: That's not my intention, I assure you. I humbly beg that you forgive me.

BARTOLOME: Then why?

FRAY ANTONIO: Because my conscience prevents me from absolving someone who lacks the desire to reform. And although you are repentant about the past and affected by the death of your friend, you, Bartolomé de Las Casas, you do not sorrow for the present or the future of these children of God.

BARTOLOME: You have made a grave mistake with me, Fray Antonio Montesinos. I am a proud man and a bad enemy.

FRAY ANTONIO: And I am a poor friar who cannot forsake the thorny duty of proclaiming my convictions...to you and to the whole colony, no matter what the price I must pay. (*BARTOLOME has exited. FRAY ANTONIO slowly climbs the stairs to the upper stage. Once there, he unfurls a red brocade to form a pulpit. Simultaneously, on the lower stage, there is the red glow of fire, the sound of weapons, gunshots, and screams.*) "Ego vox clamantis in deserto." I am the voice that clamors in the wilderness. The sermon for the first Sunday of Advent, in the Year of our Lord 1511. Let us pray. (*He kneels and prays as the action continues on the lower stage. Enter BARTOLOME and PEDRO RENTERIA.*)

BARTOLOME (*In different clothes*): What's happening?

PEDRO RENTERIA: Oh, Bartolomé, it's an inferno. They are knifing and killing all the Indians that were in the square to see the soldiers' horses.

BARTOLOME: But why?

PEDRO RENTERIA: One devil, to test the sharpness of his sword, started swinging it against the natives. As they fled screaming, the others chased them, and faster than you could say two "Our Fathers," no one was left, not an old man, not a child.

BARTOLOME: Oh my God! Let's go...

GABRIEL (*Entering*): No, nephew. It's an orgy of blood. They are drunk, as if it were a great battle.

PEDRO RENTERIA: Against a flock of defenseless lambs.

GABRIEL: Even I caught their madness. God forgive me. Look. My sword is covered with innocent blood.

BARTOLOME: Good Lord!

(*BARTOLOME and PEDRO RENTERIA exit, followed by GABRIEL.*)

FRAY ANTONIO: So that you may know, I have come to this pulpit, and the voice shall be the harshest and most frightening that you have ever thought to hear. And this voice says to you, those in authority and colonists of this island, that you are all in mortal sin. In mortal sin you live and die for the cruelty and tyranny with which you treat these poor children of God.

(*BARTOLOME has entered, carrying a wounded Indian woman in his arms. PEDRO RENTERIA and GABRIEL also appear.*)

BARTOLOME: God be praised. The wound is not deep.

PEDRO RENTERIA: Stabbed, disemboweled, they flee in terror, holding their guts in their hands.

GABRIEL: Stop whimpering like a woman.

BARTOLOME (*To Gabriel*): Bring me some strips of cloth so I can stop the bleeding. (*To Pedro Rentrería.*) And water to baptize this poor woman.

(*Exit GABRIEL and PEDRO RENTERIA. BARTOLOME lays the Indian woman down on the floor.*)

FRAY ANTONIO: On what authority do you make such despicable war against these meek and pacific people who were here on their own lands?

PEDRO RENTERIA: The stream flows red with blood.

FRAY ANTONIO: Are they not men? Do they not have rational souls?

BARTOLOME (*Baptizing the woman while PEDRO RENTERIA kneels at his side*): I baptize you María, in the name of the Father, the Son, and the Holy Ghost.

FRAY ANTONIO: Are you not obliged to love them as you love yourselves?

MARIA-INDIAN: Zabai, zabai...

BARTOLOME: Do not cry, woman. Have no fear. There will be no more...

PEDRO RENTERIA: They killed her brother and her father when they were bringing bread and fish to the troops.

GOVERNOR (*Entering*): Put your arms away! Form your companies!

PEDRO RENTERIA (*Standing up*): Governor, Your Excellency.

FRAY ANTONIO: You may be certain that in your present condition you have no more possibility of salvation than do the Arabs and the Turks who know of but reject the faith.

GOVERNOR (*To Bartolomé*): And what do you think of the atrocity that our men have committed?

BARTOLOME: That I would send them and you to the devil!

FRAY ANTONIO: As long as you do not change your conduct toward our Indian brothers, the friars of this convent will refuse you confession as if you were highway bandits.

GOVERNOR: We are all dismayed and regret the sad events of this day.

FRAN ANTONIO: Any and all of you may write to Spain to whomever you wish!

(*GABRIEL enters with the bandages.*)

GABRIEL: The soldiers have gone wild. They're attacking the hut where a hundred or more Indians have taken refuge.

GOVERNOR: The cursed mob!

BARTOLOME (*To Pedro Rentería*): Take care of her.

(*The GOVERNOR, BARTOLOME, and GABRIEL exit. PEDRO RENTERIA tends to the woman's wounds.*)

FRAY ANTONIO: And I swear before God that nothing and no one will make me change my stance as long as you hold those brothers in such cruel and horrible servitude. Bendicat vos omnipotent Deus. (*He blesses them and with great dignity descends from the pulpit. Gregorian music. PEDRO DE CORDOBA is waiting for him. In a state of collapse, he speaks to Pedro de Córdoba.*) Pedro, I feel sick.

PEDRO DE CORDOBA: And I feel proud of you, my brother. Don't weaken. (*He puts his arm around Fray Antonio's shoulders and helps him to exit.*)

(*On stage, PEDRO LAS CASAS, GABRIEL, PETRILLA, PEDRO RENTERIA, and BARTOLOME, surrounding the GOVERNOR.*)

PEDRO LAS CASAS: That sermon was an insult to Admiral Columbus and to all those who gave their blood to bring Christianity to this land.

GABRIEL: He should be jailed for sedition.

GOVERNOR: Unfortunately, the civil authorities have no control over priests. Were it not so, he would have been arrested right in the chapel.

PETRILLA: Didn't they bring him here so he could say mass and give the Christian sacraments? Isn't that his work? Well then, he should do his work!

GABRIEL: Forgive my wife, Governor. She just arrived on the last expedition from Seville.

PETRILLA: We were married a month ago. No sooner did I land than, hurry up! Let's get to church! He's an eager one. If he'd gotten me to bed first, he wouldn't have gotten married.

GABRIEL: What does this matter to them?

PETRILLA: As one of the women at the tavern used to say, men are like iron. You have to strike while they're hot. If you let them cool down...!

GABRIEL: Shut up already!

PETRILLA: My God, can't one say anything?

GOVERNOR: That friar can sink the island in a bloodbath.

PEDRO LAS CASAS: An Indian rebellion?

GOVERNOR: Why not, if the Church incites them to it? But I am confident I can resolve the problem by talking to him calmly. I've ordered Fray Antonio to come here.

BARTOLOME: There is no one more fanatical and stubborn than he.

PEDRO RENTERIA (*To Bartolomé*): You and I witnessed the slaughter at Caonao.

BARTOLOME: But it is unjust that we should all be measured by the same standard.

PEDRO RENTERIA: I feel guilty just for having been there.

PETRILLA (*To Pedro Rentería*): What are you? A traitor?

PEDRO RENTERIA: Señora!

PETRILLA: He's married to one of them.

GABRIEL: My wife is right. Whose side are you on?

PEDRO RENTERIA: That of Her Highness Queen Isabella, may she rest in peace. In her last will and testament she commanded justice for all of her subjects, of both races.

(*Enter FRAY ANTONIO and PEDRO DE CORDOBA.*)

GOVERNOR: I only sent for Fray Antonio.

PEDRO DE CORDOBA: I am the father superior of the convent and therefore responsible for all of my friars.

GOVERNOR: As you know, the *encomienda* was instituted so that the Indians would be grouped in villages, under the authority of a Spaniard, for their protection and to teach them Christianity.

PEDRO DE CORDOBA: But you know, Governor, that the system has only made the greedy rich and incited wars of conquest to replace the Indians who die exhausted from overwork.

BARTOLOME: Fray Pedro, you know us. Do you believe that the treatment given the natives by my father, or by me, or by so many others deserves such harsh criticism? What more can they ask of us?

PEDRO DE CORDOBA: Liberty.

GABRIEL: For what? For idol worship, or slothfulness, or unspeakable vices?

PEDRO DE CORDOBA: Liberty to accept our life and our beliefs freely, without having their men turned into beasts of burden and their women into prostitutes.

GOVERNOR: That's enough! Fray Pedro, and you, Fray Antonio, I command you, in next Sunday's sermon, to retract your unwise and abusive threat.

FRAY ANTONIO: With the Father Superior's permission, allow me to say that I am not a reed to be bent by the wind. I cannot retract my words nor change my attitude whether I am commanded to by the Governor or by the King himself.

GABRIEL: He's a rebel.

FRAY ANTONIO: Of course you can imprison me or execute me. That way you can silence my voice, but you cannot open my confessional.

BARTOLOME: You do not have the right to do this moral violence to your parishioners.

FRAY ANTONIO: The Lord used a whip to drive the animal traders out of the temple. How can I fail to drive out the traders in human beings?

GOVERNOR (*To Fray Pedro*): Order your friar to come to his senses.

PEDRO DE CORDOBA: I am not a reed to be bent by the wind either, your Excellency.

GOVERNOR (*Furious*): You will be tried and expulsed from the order and excommunicated!

FRAY ANTONIO: Victims bring no honor to either country or church.

GOVERNOR: Throw them out of here!

FRAY ANTONIO: On the contrary, true glory comes only from justice.

GOVERNOR: Throw them out! (*Exit FRAY ANTONIO and PEDRO DE CORDOBA.*) I shall send a report to the King in the next mail. With a document signed by all of the colonists on the island asking that these agitators be punished as an example. Your signature, Bartolomé de Las Casas, shall head the list. You are going to be the first priest ordained in these lands and you should be the model. (*He exits.*)

PEDRO RENTERIA (*To Bartolomé*): Have you forgotten Caonao?

BARTOLOME (*Confused and in a bad mood*): No, damnation, I have not forgotten. (*He is left alone. We hear the sound of Señor's flute.*)

(*Bartolomé's plantation. MARIA crosses to Bartolomé, who remains immersed in thought.*)

MARIA: What does my master seek in the waters of the river? You spend hours watching it flow by.

BARTOLOME: I'm trying to discover my own thoughts before the current carries them away. But I am not your master.

MARIA: I shall always be your servant, ever since you and Pedro saved my life at Caonao.

BARTOLOME: You are Pedro's wife, and he is my best friend.

MARIA: Sometimes I feel guilty for being so happy.

BARTOLOME: Why?

MARIA: As if I had betrayed the memory of my people. Of my brother, my father, of all those who died in that insane slaughter.

BARTOLOME: Let us hope it never happens again.

MARIA: My grandfather was a chieftain with many huts and warriers. I can still remember when he called his tribes together to announce the arrival of some bearded men mounted on sacred animals called horses. In exchange for the peace and love they were bringing us, he was prepared to deliver everything: our lands, our maidens. And shortly afterward they were all sacrificed! There are moments when I almost forget and I think of myself as one of you...but I am not now and can never be one of you.

BARTOLOME: I would like to show you something, María. (*He shows her the charm Señor gave him that he wears hanging from his neck.*)

MARIA: But you are not from the Arawak tribe! Were you by chance married to a Zailo woman?

BARTOLOME: No.

MARIA: Then you must take that off your neck immediately.

BARTOLOME: I promised...a person who died...that I would wear it always.

MARIA: It's a terrible sin, according to the old beliefs. That person must have loved you very much. Only the Arawaks and their mates are allowed to wear it.

BARTOLOME: I don't believe in idols. (*He puts the charm back and continues to look at the river. The GOVERNOR enters and sits down at his desk.*)

GOVERNOR (*To Bartolomé*): Come in, my dear Bartolomé, and wait just a moment.

BARTOLOME (*To María*): I asked for an audience with the Governor.

GOVERNOR (To Bartolomé): I'm very pleased to see you again.

MARIA (*To Bartolomé*): What are you asking the Governor for?

BARTOLOME (*To María*): Nothing. On the contrary, I am the one who is going to give him something.

GOVERNOR (*To Bartolomé*): I'm listening.

BARTOLOME (*To the Governor*): I cannot become rich from something that does not belong to me.

GOVERNOR (*To Bartolomé*): And why not, if I, in the name of the Crown, have granted it to you?

BARTOLOME (*To the Governor*): Because it does not belong to you either, and I fear that it also does not belong to the Crown.

GOVERNOR (*To Bartolomé*): Have you lost your mind?

BARTOLOME (*To the Governor*): At the time of the Dominicans' sermon I felt insulted, and I did what I could to make them understand their error. But as I continue to reflect, I find that my arguments have vanished. Do you know why, your Excellency? Because they were right, and we were wrong.

GOVERNOR (*To Bartolomé*): But the New Laws...

BARTOLOME (*To the Governor*): They have not improved the situation of these unfortunate people one iota. They are forced to work from sun to sun for a pittance and the smallest ration of food that will keep them working.

GOVERNOR (*To Bartolomé*): Their lot will soon improve.

BARTOLOME (*To the Governor*): "Later, but not now." That's what we always say to them. But the only life they have is now.

GOVERNOR (*To Bartolomé*): And eternal life.

BARTOLOME (*To the Governor*): Christ was not satisfied with just that.

GOVERNOR (*To Bartolomé*): What can you do?

BARTOLOME (*To the Governor*): The only thing that is in my power. Renounce the Indians you entrusted to me, your Excellency.

GOVERNOR: Do you realize the seriousness of such a gesture? (*He turns toward a large window upstage.*)

MARIA (*To Bartolomé*): Who will be assigned the Indians that you renounce?

BARTOLOME (*To María*): The Governor will decide.

MARIA (*To Bartolomé*): But the treatment they will receive will be less humane than yours.

BARTOLOME (*To María*): I know, but what can I do, María? How can I convince anyone otherwise if I am taking advantage of them?

MARIA (*To Bartolomé*): This could make enemies for you among all of them, Indians and Spaniards.

GOVERNOR (*To Bartolomé*): I should punish you.

BARTOLOME (*To the Governor*): For what crime?

GOVERNOR (*To Bartolomé*): We'll find one. Then as a sanction I can take away your Indians. That way you can have your wish without provoking anyone.

BARTOLOME (*To the Governor*): I want to renounce them voluntarily.

GOVERNOR (*To Bartolomé*): Do you realize what you're saying? You not only want to separate yourself from your Indians. That's not enough for you! You want to turn this into a political banner, against the laws of the Crown. And that is a crime.

BARTOLOME (*To the Governor*): I'm going to sell all of my possessions to pay my passage to Spain. I shall ask for an audience with the King.

GOVERNOR (*To Bartolomé*): I should stop you.

BARTOLOME: No one can prohibit me from seeing the King. (*Handing him a document.*) My renunciation.

GOVERNOR (*To Bartolomé*): Go to the devil, Bartolomé de Las Casas!

MARIA (*To Bartolomé*): May the Lord bless your noble gesture.

(*Exit MARIA.*)

GOVERNOR: And who will work the land and the mines if they all renounce their Indians like you? We'd end up importing blacks, from the Portuguese markets.

BARTOLOME: If that's what it takes to save the Indians.

GOVERNOR: And waste our gold on foreign merchandise, when here we have it free?... God be with you!

BARTOLOME (*Exiting*): The document...

GOVERNOR: Leave it on the desk, or wherever in hell you please.

(*The port, in 1515. The deck of the ship on which Bartolomé will sail. PEDRO LAS CASAS, PEDRO RENTERIA, MARIA, GABRIEL, and PETRILLA come to say goodbye. BARTOLOME enters, dressed as a priest.*)

BARTOLOME: Thank you, Father, for coming to say goodbye to me.

PEDRO LAS CASAS: I've put two small bags of gold in your baggage: one for your mother and one for your sister. Tell them that I am well and think of them.

BARTOLOME: I would have liked to take them a letter from you.

PEDRO LAS CASAS: One of these days I'm going to write them, I promise.
BARTOLOME: Or better yet, you could have joined me on this voyage.
PEDRO LAS CASAS: Impossible.
BARTOLOME: You still have time. I can arrange it for you in a wink.
PEDRO LAS CASAS: Here comes your uncle Gabriel.

(*Enter GABRIEL and PETRILLA.*)

GABRIEL: I'm angry with you, nephew. But Petrilla insisted on coming.
PETRILLA: So you can make peace before he leaves.
GABRIEL: Renouncing your Indians is an affront to the rest of us. Worse
    yet, it's stupid.
PETRILLA: It seems strange to me to see you like that, in those clothes.
GABRIEL: You're a clever one. You had your fun first, and now you're a
    priest.
MARIA: Is it true that you will see the King himself?
BARTOLOME: That's my intention.
PEDRO RENTERIA: I'm talking about schools. We have to teach the
    children to read and to study the true faith.
PEDRO LAS CASAS: Look who's coming.

(*Enter FRAY ANTONIO and PEDRO DE CORDOBA.*)

GABRIEL: Are you going to Spain with those renegades?
PEDRO RENTERIA: Everyone says they're saints.
GABRIEL: Traitors, that's what they are. An insult to decent people.

(*PEDRO DE CORDOBA says goodbye to FRAY ANTONIO at the foot of
the stairs.*)

FRAY ANTONIO: You ought to go. I am not worthy of such a sensitive
    mission. I do not have the gift of convincing people.
PEDRO DE CORDOBA: When you feel weak, think of your Indian
    brothers and of the suffering of Christ in the garden.

(*FRAY ANTONIO embraces PEDRO DE CORDOBA and boards the
ship.*)

GABRIEL: They're starting to weigh anchor. You have to get on board,
    Bartolomé.
BARTOLOME (*To Pedro Las Casas*): Goodbye, Father.
PEDRO LAS CASAS: Come back soon.
GABRIEL: And you, aren't you going to kiss your nephew's hand? His hand
    or whatever...there's no longer any danger I suppose! (*He laughs.*)
PETRILLA (*To Gabriel*): I'd like to speak for a moment with Bartolomé.

GABRIEL: What do you have to tell him?

PETRILLA: What difference does it make to you! (*They withdraw from the group.*)

BARTOLOME: What is it?

PETRILLA: I'm going to have a baby.

BARTOLOME: What wonderful news! Does your husband know?

PETRILLA: I'm very frightened.

BARTOLOME: Why?

PETRILLA: I don't know who the father is. Maybe it's Gabriel, and maybe it's one of the others...and in that case, the color of its skin will be an unmistakable accusation.

BARTOLOME: My God.

PETRILLA: Our house is a real brothel, Bartolomé. There's not an Indian woman, young or old, who hasn't been in his bed. Sometimes he makes me watch, or he gags the unfortunate husband and puts him under the bed so he can hear everything. That way he increases his own pleasure.

BARTOLOME: I can't believe you.

PETRILLA: There's not one man who's free of that sin. They're all the same with the women. Why should it be surprising that I, too, like to give pleasure to my body once in a while? I'm not made of ice, you'll remember.

BARTOLOME: But now you're a respectable lady.

PETRILLA: And he's a gentleman. Although that wouldn't stop him from killing it. The life of a newborn mestizo will be no more valuable to him than that of any Indian.

BARTOLOME: How could you think such a thing?

PETRILLA: I know him better than you, and he's capable of anything. But I'm going to stop it, one way or another. I'll give birth in secret, and I'll tell him that it was born dead, and I'll give my baby to some native women to take care of. Only you will know of its existence.

BARTOLOME: Trust God.

PETRILLA: I trust you, Bartolomé, only you.

GABRIEL (*Approaching*): What secrets do you have with the priest?

PETRILLA (*To Gabriel*): Leave me in peace! (*To Bartolomé*) I wish you were the father. There was a time when you could have been.

BARTOLOME: Have mercy.

PETRILLA: I didn't mean to offend you. On the contrary, I thought you would be happy to know that in spite of your priest's robes, you're still a man. (*The ship's bell sounds again.*)

GABRIEL: Get up there! Hurry!

PETRILLA (To *Bartolomé*): If it's a boy, I'll name him Señor. Like the little Indian who used to wait under the window when you and I were in my bed.

VOICES: Weigh anchor!

BARTOLOME (*Getting on board, he takes leave of them all by making the sign of the cross*): May the Lord bless you all!
VOICES: Set sail!

(*The group on land saying goodbye to the ship begins to move upstage as the light comes down. MARIA takes out a handkerchief. The others wave their lariats. BARTOLOME and FRAY ANTONIO are on the ship deck. Sounds of the sea and of seagulls.*)

BARTOLOME: We meet again, Fray Antonio.
FRAY ANTONIO: Are you still angry at me?
BARTOLOME: I must admit that your Advent sermon...did not lack courage.
FRAY ANTONIO: Nor did you, when you returned your Indians to the Governor.
VOICES: On the bow, ahoy!
FRAY ANTONIO: If your conscience needs it, now I would like to give you the absolution you once asked me for.
BARTOLOME: Have you hear me in confession? I'd rather be condemned for all eternity.
VOICES: Tie off the mizzen!
FRAY ANTONIO: I hear that you intend to see the King as I do.
BARTOLOME: I have written a major reorganizational plan for the colony.
FRAY ANTONIO: I only wish to improve the lives of my Indian parishioners.
BARTOLOME: You're content with very little. You'll always be a poor friar.
FRAY ANTONIO: And you, a proud and ambitious man.
VOICES: Tie off the mainsail!
FRAY ANTONIO: Since the two of us are going to the royal court and the trip will be a long one, what do you say we declare a truce?
BARTOLOME: Just temporarily.
FRAY ANTONIO: It's agreed then, Bartolomé de Las Casas?
BARTOLOME: Agreed, Antonio de Montesinos. (*They shake hands ceremoniously.*)
VOICES: Ahoy! Ahoy! Ahoy!

END OF THE SECOND ACT

ACT III

Seville, 1515. Evening in the home of the Las Casas family. The table is set for one person. Isabel-Daughter is next to the window. Isabel-Mother enters.

ISABEL-MOTHER: Hasn't Bartolomé come back yet?

ISABEL-DAUGHTER: What are you doing out of bed? You know the doctor's orders.

ISABEL-MOTHER: Do you think something's happened to him?

ISABEL-DAUGHTER: Since he's come back from the Indies he's very busy with his affairs.

ISABEL-MOTHER: But the streets of Seville are filled with beggars and dangerous people, and Bartolomé has many enemies. Heat up the kettle. He'll be coming soon. Are the girls asleep?

ISABEL-DAUGHTER: For almost an hour.

ISABEL-MOTHER: This has become a house without men. You're a widow, your father is far away, with Uncle Gabriel. We have only Bartolomé left, and he's always traveling, with his baggage always ready to leave us again.

ISABEL-DAUGHTER: I don't need anybody to help me run our little business.

ISABEL-MOTHER: You called me a wet blanket because I was not overjoyed at the discovery of that new world. But the years have passed and now you see that I was right. Here the Royal Court and its officials have gotten rich, but the rest of us are as poor as ever.

ISABEL-DAUGHTER: And what of the good we do for the savages who do not believe in God?

ISABEL-MOTHER: And the harm, my dear. Because when they talk about what goes on there...

ISABEL-DAUGHTER: Do you remember Señor? He became a Christian.

ISABEL-MOTHER: And they rewarded him by working him to death.

ISABEL-DAUGHTER: Everything's going to change, Mother. Sometimes when Bartolomé and that friar talk about all of their efforts to see the King, I feel as if a fresh breeze has entered the house.

ISABEL-MOTHER: What can a poor priest do against the rich and powerful?

ISABEL-DAUGHTER: He will succeed.

ISABEL-MOTHER: He has no sense. He risks his life to make his fortune and then he gives back his earnings to turn himself into a redeemer.

ISABEL-DAUGHTER: And don't you feel proud, Mother?

ISABEL-MOTHER: No, not when your daughters lack the basic essentials.

ISABEL-DAUGHTER: What difference does that make!

BARTOLOME (*Entering*): Good evening.

ISABEL-MOTHER: Isabel will get you your supper.

BARTOLOME: I'm not hungry.

ISABEL-MOTHER: You'll get sick. You're thin, and you have bags under your eyes.

BARTOLOME: I'm very upset. Everything that's going on in the New World has its roots here. The officials at the Spanish House of Trade are supposed to be protecting the Indians but they're only interested in gold, silver, and selling slaves.

ISABEL-MOTHER: How's the soup? I put in a ham bone to give it flavor.

BARTOLOME: Of the grievances sent in writing, the Royal Court receives only the ones that suit their interests. The others can rot in the files.

ISABEL-MOTHER: Give him some bread crumbs for the soup, Isabel.

BARTOLOME: They allocate Indians to people who have never even set foot on those lands. In exchange for bribes, they grant Indians to whomever they please. They collect for their favors and they leave their enemies destitute. Bishop Fonseca and Secretary Conchillos are the ones responsible for such widespread corruption.

ISABEL-MOTHER: Be quiet. Don't even mention their names. They can punish at whim. All Seville knows that.

BARTOLOME: I'm not afraid of them. I shall tell His Majesty what's going on in his kingdom.

ISABEL-MOTHER: That's if he finally agrees to see you.

ISABEL-DAUGHTER: You've been trying for months.

BARTOLOME: But the King needs me. He is isolated on his throne. He needs my truth just as much as his vassals do on the other side of the sea.

ISABEL-MOTHER: You are unbearably vain.

FRAY ANTONIO (*Entering*): Forgive the lateness of the hour, but I couldn't wait to tell you the good news.

BARTOLOME: Has it come?

FRAY ANTONIO: Here's the notice that the Father Superior just gave me at the convent. The King has granted us an audience next Tuesday.

BARTOLOME: Bring us some wine, Isabel, so that we may celebrate such joyous news.

FRAY ANTONIO: It would be better to give thanks to God.

BARTOLOME: There is no conflict between wine and prayer, Fray Antonio. The mass teaches us that. Let us drink to His Majesty, King Ferdinand the Catholic.

(*BARTOLOME drinks from the jug brought by ISABEL-DAUGHTER. FRAY ANTONIO does not drink.*)

FRAY ANTONIO: It is against the rules of my convent.

BARTOLOME: The rules do not foresee occasions like this one. Oh, Fray Antonio, you can be exasperating at even the happiest of moments. Don't take the jug away, Isabel. I'm not a Dominican. (*He takes another drink.*)

FRAY ANTONIO: Do you have the memorial ready to present to the King?

BARTOLOME: With irrefutable evidence. I assure you that he will be moved by such a well-documented accusation.

FRAY ANTONIO: If he's in any condition to be moved.

BARTOLOME: I don't understand.

FRAY ANTONIO: His Majesty is ill and they fear for his life.

BARTOLOME: Oh, no. God cannot play such a trick on us. Pray, Fray Antonio. Pray night and day that the Lord grant him life long enough that he may hear our grievances and remedy so many ills.

FRAY ANTONIO: His will be done. (*To Isabel-Mother*). I ask again that you pardon me, Señora.

ISABEL-MOTHER: In exchange, would you do me a great favor?

FRAY ANTONIO: Of course.

ISABEL-MOTHER: Then tell my son not to give up eating. He's turning into skin and bones.

(*Enter SECRETARY CONCHILLOS. We are in the outer chamber of King Ferdinand. Conchillos is an enigmatic figure. His head is shaven and he has no eyebrows--like a reptile.*)

CONCHILLOS (*Calling them*): Father Bartolomé de Las Casas and Fray Antonio Montesinos. (*They both cross to him.*) Welcome.

BARTOLOME: This is the memorandum in which His Majesty grants us an audience.

CONCHILLOS: I recognize it. I was the one responsible for its delivery. But His Majesty has had a setback and is in no condition to consider questions of state.

BARTOLOME: We are to see the King.

CONCHILLOS: By virtue of my post, I can decide any matter related to the Indies. Speak.

FRAY ANTONIO: Señor Conchillos, sir, as Secretary of the Council of the Indies you cannot be unaware of the disastrous situation of the native vassals across the sea.

CONCHILLOS: I am aware of their suffering and am in solidarity with your noble attitude.

BARTOLOME: Then what people say about you is false?

CONCHILLOS: No one is free of slander and envy.

BARTOLOME: Is it not true that you claim the privilege of branding the slaves and receive a fee for each one?

CONCHILLOS: Slavery of insurgents and rebels is permitted throughout the civilized world.

BARTOLOME: Have you been granted 100 Indians on Hispaniola and another 200 in Cuba, who work and die while you get rich? Do you sell royal favor and hold up the papers of those who are not generous with you?

CONCHILLOS: You have a loose tongue, Father Bartolomé. I am a good friend to my friends when it comes to awarding favors and repaying loyalty. But in spite of my natural goodness, I am implacable with enemies and traitors.

BARTOLOME: Friendship or emnity between men depends upon the cause they defend.

CONCHILLOS: Of course. And I wish to reward the nobleness of your cause. Fray Antonio, I am aware of the poverty of your convent in Santo Domingo. I shall sign an order for 800 gold coins in order to renovate your chapel. As for you, my dear Father Bartolomé, I shall see that in the next allocation you are granted a large enough number of Indians so that you may devote yourself, without economic hardship, to your commendable endeavors as an evangelist.

BARTOLOME: I renounced my Indians before I left.

CONCHILLOS: In that case, tell me what I can do for our friendship.

BARTOLOME: Take me to the King.

CONCHILLOS: And you, Fray Antonio, what do you think of my offer?

FRAY ANTONIO: Give the 800 gold coins to the impoverished Indians.

CONCHILLOS: You two are in agreement. Bravo! In that case, speak with his excellency Bishop Fonseca.

(*FONSECA has entered. He has an impenetrably stern look.*)

FONSECA: What do you wish from His Majesty?

BARTOLOME: I wish to present him this memorial with fourteen resolutions for the Reform of the Indies.

FONSECA: I am Governor General of those lands. Give it to me.

BARTOLOME: We will give it only to the King himself.

FRAY ANTONIO: The cruel treatment is so extreme that the Indians are perishing before we can even convert them to Christianty.

FONSECA: They have a weak nature and are subject to disease.

BARTOLOME: Bishop Fonseca, I witnessed the slaughter at Caonao.

FONSECA: For our government, the affairs of state are serious and difficult. What difference can it make to me, or to the King, what happens to some ignorant idol-worshippers?

BARTOLOME: So it makes no difference either to your honor or to the King that those poor souls are dying? Great God in Heaven. To whom should it make a difference then? Come, Fray Antonio, I cannot bear such cynicism.

FONSECA: What insolence!

CONCHILLOS: He's out of his mind.

FONSECA: Father Bartolomé. And you, friar. Stop. You shall see the King. Dead or alive. But you will never be able to say that Bishop Fonseca prevented you from doing so for fear of your insidious fantasies. Follow me. I shall take you to the royal chamber.

(They climb to the upper stage where FONSECA draws open the curtains of the royal bed. KING FERDINAND THE CATHOLIC appears. He is old and ill, and suffers from edema, but retains the bright and astute look of the Renaissance prince.)

KING: What's happening?

FONSECA: An audience, Señor.

KING: I don't want to see anyone! I can barely move my body. My mind is clouded over and my arms are falling off. I don't give a fig for any earthly or heavenly matter.

FONSECA *(Ironically)*: Two of your subjects from across the sea bring you grand and marvelous resolutions for changing policy on those islands, my Lord.

KING: When I can scarcely breathe and my guts are cutting into my throat like a dagger, I assure you that I couldn't care less about issues in the Indies. Can't we leave it for tomorrow?

FONSECA: I'm afraid not, Majesty. They're very obstinate.

KING: Speak.

BARTOLOME: Not in front of them.

KING: Do you think you own the palace? *(To Fonseca and Conchillos.)* Leave us alone. *(FONSECA and CONCHILLOS descend to the lower stage where they listen to what is being said up above.)* You don't trust those two? Quite right. I don't either. They're a pair of sly rogues, like most of my attendants. But I can't find any better ones. Please, the sooner you begin, the sooner we'll get through.

BARTOLOME: Most high and powerful King and Lord... *(He takes out a thick report.)*

KING: Good God, no. Don't read me a tome like that. Just give me a short summary.

BARTOLOME: What we presume to propose to Your Majesty, in order to counter the great ills that afflict the Crown in the New World, are fourteen resolutions.

KING *(In alarm)*: Fourteen, you say? *(He chokes in fright.)* Oh, oh, oh...

FRAY ANTONIO: What's wrong, Your Majesty?

KING: I'm choking. Give me that green potion and a jug of water. *(FRAY ANTONIO gives it to him and the King drinks.)* Oh, oh. *(Feeling better.)* What resolution are you on?

BARTOLOME: Señor, I have not yet begun.

KING: The doctors who tend me are a bunch of quacks. They're killing me with their concoctions and their bloodletting. But they won't get away with it. I'm the King and I'll not die until it suits my royal pleasure. Proceed.

BARTOLOME: In the first place, the forced labor of the Indians on the *encomiendas* must be abolished.

FONSECA: And how are the colonists going to pay taxes?

CONCHILLOS: Who's ever heard of curing ills with idleness?

BARTOLOME: Having Indians to labor until they die from exhaustion cannot be the reward given to discoverers and conquistadors.

FONSECA: He's against private property.

CONCHILLOS: And free competition.

BARTOLOME: If they are all your vassals, Señor, both Spaniards and Indians, let them share the fruits of their labors like brothers.

FONSECA: That would be the last straw!

BARTOLOME: United and free, in time the sons and daughters of them both will come together and form a new people.

CONCHILLOS: A race of halfbreeds, God only knows of what color.

FONSECA: And before you know it, they'll want their independence from the Crown. Heaven help us!

KING: And what would I gain from that?

BARTOLOME: The gratitude of an entire race...and the taxes from your new subjects.

KING: That's not bad.

BARTOLOME: Give me a thousand leagues along the coast, my Lord. A territory, in Tierra Firme, where I can found a model colony, based on justice, that will provide you with 15,000 ducats of income by the third year, and 30,000 the sixth year, and 60,000 the tenth year.

KING: Do you think that's possible?

FONSECA: Did you hear that, Conchillos? He's just another ambitious politician.

BARTOLOME: A place to convince, not to conquer, where the word and truth prevail instead of force. Only friars and peaceful farmers. No soldiers, no guardhouses, no greed. So that they may voluntarily accept our faith and our Empire.

FRAY ANTONIO: Father Bartolomé. The King is not listening to you. He isn't moving or breathing.

BARTOLOME: Majesty! Your Majesty!

FRAY ANTONIO (*Calling for help*): Hello there, you, in the palace! The King! The King!

BARTOLOME: My God! (*FONSECA and CONCHILLOS quickly climb the stairs.*)

CONCHILLOS: Señor, Señor... Heaven help us, he's dead.

FONSECA: What did you do to His Majesty?

FRAY ANTONIO: Father Bartolomé was explaining his doctrine to him.

FONSECA: What terrible assertions does that document contain that could cause a king's death? You shall answer to the authorities for this!

BARTOLOME: That's a false accusation.

FONSECA: The King is dead. Long live the King!

CONCHILLOS: Excuse me, Bishop, but I believe his heart is still beating.

FONSECA: Call the royal doctors.

KING: No, not that! I won't have it! Throw them out of the Court immediately!

FONSECA: Majesty!

KING: And don't be in such a hurry to announce my death. I haven't lost all my wind yet. As for you (*To Bartolomé*), your proposition does not displease me. Did you say 60,000 ducats?

BARTOLOME: Within ten years.

FRAY ANTONIO: By improving the lot of the Indian.

KING: We wouldn't lose anything by trying. In a short while, the Court will be leaving for Seville. I shall await you there.

BARTOLOME: Thank you, Your Majesty.

FRAY ANTONIO: We kiss your hand.

KING: The audience has ended.

(*FRAY ANTONIO and BARTOLOME go down the steps and remain on the lower stage.*)

CONCHILLOS: Permit me to express our happiness, my Lord, at your excellent health.

KING: Don't be an idiot. My health is as bad as ever.

FONSECA: Did you wish something else from your obedient servants?

KING: Get me something to eat. Some green beans and some pork. I'm hungry.

FONSECA: Legumes bloat your stomach, my Lord.

KING: It's these concoctions and ointments those doctors brewed up that have made me like this. Get out! Everybody out! (*With a sweep of his hand, he knocks all of the medicines from his table to the floor.*)

FONSECA: At your service, Señor. (*He draws the curtains across the bed and exits with Conchillos.*)

(*FRAY ANTONIO and BARTOLOME are traveling along the road to Seville. Perhaps they are on mules, from which they dismount at once. It is night.*)

BARTOLOME: Have you been asleep?

FRAY ANTONIO: I was praying.

BARTOLOME: Don't you ever stop praying? I was dreaming.

FRAY ANTONIO: And you, don't you ever stop dreaming?

BARTOLOME: At last the King seems ready to help us. You don't seem very pleased.

FRAY ANTONIO: I am. But as soon as we reach Seville, I'm going to start arranging to return to Santo Domingo.

BARTOLOME: You're going to leave me here by myself?

FRAY ANTONIO: You continue to think just like a conquistador, Bartolomé. With a thousand miles of land under your control. You want your own little empire.

BARTOLOME: For our King, to whom the Pope has granted the grave responsibility of peacefully converting the pagans to Christianity.

FRAY ANTONIO: You speak of ducats and tribute.

BARTOLOME: That's the only language they understand here.

FRAY ANTONIO: The King exists for the people, not the people to satisfy the King's greed. The road to justice cannot easily pass through avarice.

BARTOLOME: The end is just. We shall see that the means are, too.

FRAY ANTONIO: I only think about my poor parishioners, weary and ill. I see them one by one. Don't you sometimes remember that poor little Señor whom God has taken to his Glory?

BARTOLOME: I often hear the music of his flute.

FRAY ANTONIO: Thousands of Arawaks play the ancient sounds of his tribe. (*Pause, during which the sound of the flute is heard.*)

BARTOLOME: How do you expect to straighten out the wrongs? By praying?

FRAY ANTONIO: It's possible. But without twisting something else on the pretense that it can be used to right the other wrongs.

BARTOLOME: I shall wait in Seville for the arrival of the Court. And nothing and no one will prevent me from seeing the King again.

(*Bells start to peal, here and there. It is a death knell.*)

FRAY ANTONIO: Do you hear?

BARTOLOME: I'm not deaf.

FRAY ANTONIO: The bells of all the churches and chapels are tolling a death.

BARTOLOME: The King is dead.

FRAY ANTONIO: May the Lord have mercy on his soul.

(*FRAY ANTONIO kneels and prays. BARTOLOME in desperation confronts God.*)

BARTOLOME: Lord, you can't do this to me. Now when I had His Majesty on my side. Sometimes You seem as inept as Fray Antonio. Why couldn't you have kept the King alive a few more days? Long enough to get to Seville and approve my projects? You could have greatly benefitted not only the Indians but Spain herself, a country you supposedly protect. Do you know what they're going to say about us if we don't change all this?

FRAY ANTONIO: Requiem eternem dona ei Domine. Amen.

BARTOLOME: But I will not slacken my efforts. I swear to you, Lord. I shall plead my case with the Regent, with Cardinal Cisneros, with whomever I must. I'll go to Queen Joanna, however mad she may be. I'll go to Flanders to talk to Prince Charles and his coterie of advisers even if I have to learn to speak Flemish. The death of a king or of a hundred kings and chancellors is not going to deter me. And if it's this year or next year or within ten or a hundred years, some day at dawn I will return to Santo Domingo. I'll be standing on the ship's deck waving the official approval of my plan like a banner. Are you listening to me, Fray Antonio?

FRAY ANTONIO: In great bewilderment and fear.

BARTOLOME: So we have agreed to meet, you and I, on the rocks at the port.

FRAY ANTONIO: The will of God above all.

BARTOLOME: God is with us. Oh, you're still just a poor, frightened friar from Extremadura.

FRAY ANTONIO: And you are an arrogant and insolent young gentleman from Seville.

BARTOLOME: Don't forget our date.

FRAY ANTONIO: I'll be there.

(BARTOLOME rapidly climbs to the upper stage, the ship's deck. At the same time, following a solemn trumpet fanfare, PEDRO RENTERIA enters with a document in his hand that he reads in a vibrant voice.)

PEDRO RENTERIA: We hereby proclaim that no one should dare harm or in anyway interfere with the inhabitants of the so-called Pearl Coast, in the territory of Tierra Firme, which has been allocated to Father Bartolomé de Las Casas. By decree of His Majesty King Charles I. God save the King.

(Another trumpet fanfare. FRAY ANTONIO, who remains on the lower stage, approaches the upper level from which BARTOLOME speaks to him while clutching a pile of royal documents.)

BARTOLOME: Fray Antonio! Fray Antonio! *(FRAY ANTONIO waves to him from below. It is the agreed upon meeting.)* It took me five years, but here it is! Confess that you never believed I could achieve it. These are the agreements signed by our young King in order to found a Model Colony, where there will be neither soldiers nor owners of Indian laborers. Just peaceful farmers who will join us from Castile. Here it all is, in my hand, and right under your nose, Fray Antonio!

(FRAY PEDRO DE CORDOBA immediately joins FRAY ANTONIO. BARTOLOME descends the stairs to embrace them, but the friars, who have greeted him coldly with a nod of their heads, exit. Bartolomé is left alone, bewildered, with the papers in his hand. Enter MARIA, PEDRO

LAS CASAS, and PEDRO RENTERIA with a table bearing the sign: "Company for the Peaceful Colonization of the Coast.")

PEDRO RENTERIA: Twenty ounces of gold.
MARIA: Three silver ingots, 120 ducats, and 98 Castilians.
PEDRO LAS CASAS: A miserable capital for such a costly enterprise.

(Enter PETRILLA on the upper stage, where she sings and dances.)

PETRILLA *(Singing)*: The evening time in Seville, Seville,
    How far away it seems,
    There's no jasmin here; only my sorrow,
    And tears from broken dreams.
    Perhaps I'm rich and envied by some,
    It's all the same to me.
    I'd trade it all for a single day
    When I could happy be.

PEDRO RENTERIA: But aren't there fifty Spaniards of good will on this island who want to join such a praiseworthy venture?
PEDRO LAS CASAS: There are no spoils of war or slaves for them to gain here.
PEDRO RENTERIA: Not even the colonists who were supposed to come from Castile. The masters there don't want their serfs to become free men.
MARIA: But Father Bartolomé will not let these difficulties defeat him.
PETRILLA *(Singing on the upper stage)*:
    In my soul there is a wound, a wound,
    A never-healing sore.
    A son sent off to the hinterlands,
    Whom I saw never more.
    I am no wife nor widow either.
    The years I've left are few.
    If only I were a girl again,
    To start my life anew.

BARTOLOME *(Entering)*: I've asked a moneylender for a sizable sum so we can charter the boats to take us to the coast.
PEDRO LAS CASAS: But who will even get aboard them?
BARTOLOME: There will be volunteers. Remember the parable from the Gospels. If those invited to the marriage feast do not come, let us gather at our table the lame, the felons, and the beggars. There is a general amnesty for anyone willing to evangelize the hinterlands, the Tierras Perdidas. Well then, we'll recruit our men from the jails, and taverns,

and shanties along the port. If the respectable people behave like riffraff, why then I'll turn the riffraff into respectable gentlemen.

PETRILLA (*Who has descended to the lower stage*): I bring you 200 ducats for your company.

BARTOLOME: Where did you get 200 ducats?

PETRILLA: I want to go with you to the Tierras Perdidas.

PEDRO LAS CASAS: Abandoning one's husband is a very serious crime.

PETRILLA: I'll seek protection under the general amnesty.

PEDRO LAS CASAS: There are no pardons for women or slaves. You are your husband's property and you have no rights, not even under royal favor.

PETRILLA: I hate you. I hate all of you!

(*GABRIEL enters and confronts his wife.*)

GABRIEL: You stole my 200 ducats!

PETRILLA: I've been your harlot, your servant, your scrubwoman. Isn't all that worth even 200 ducats?

GABRIEL (*Grabbing her*): Get to the kitchen!

PETRILLA: Gabriel, let me go with them. I'm no longer very young, and you get no pleasure from me. You're rich. Other women can warm your bed and tend your house.

GABRIEL: What God has joined, let no man rend asunder. That's His law. And as long as I'm alive, whether you like it or not, you'll remain at my side.

PETRILLA: I'll kill myself.

GABRIEL: Don't make me laugh. Who ever heard of a whore killing herself?

BARTOLOME: Good God, Uncle Gabriel!

GABRIEL: It's not in your interests to tangle with me, Bartolomé. It may be that the outcome of your worthless venture is in my hands.

BARTOLOME: We don't need you.

GABRIEL: You're mistaken. Your moneylender is demanding security on your loan that nobody will give you if I don't. Besides, I can supply you with boats and food and the signatures of the officials who have to give you permission to sail.

PETRILLA: Don't make deals with him. He spoils everything he touches!

GABRIEL: Shut your mouth, you harpy!

PEDRO LAS CASAS: If, with your uncle's help, we can move the company forward...

PEDRO RENTERIA: I don't like it.

MARIA: Nor do I.

GABRIEL: You understand that I am not making this offer on a personal basis. The Governor, the Treasurer, and the Purser, who up to now have been keeping you from carrying out your plan, are now ready to do business with you.

BARTOLOME: Why?

GABRIEL: You represent the authority of the Crown, and nobody wants to oppose that.

PETRILLA: Don't listen to him!

GABRIEL: Get out of my sight!

PETRILLA: I don't want to, you scoundrel!

GABRIEL: The costs of financing this will be deducted from the earnings off the land.

BARTOLOME: There will be no armed men on my lands.

GABRIEL: The troops will build their castles at the two boundaries, to provide you protection. And for the slaves.

BARTOLOME: What slaves?

GABRIEL: The fierce Carib Indians who eat human flesh and murder their neighbors. They are to be subdued, by royal order.

PEDRO RENTERIA: That's the excuse they use to make slaves of the most peaceful tribes.

BARTOLOME: I shall not fail to comply with the King's orders. But nobody will seize even one of them unless I have personally determined whether he is a dangerous enemy and eats human flesh.

GABRIEL: The Governor himself, with all the pomp that the occasion merits, will sign the agreement.

BARTOLOME: Let Petrilla join the expedition.

GABRIEL: You still want to sleep with her?

BARTOLOME: I will not allow such comments!

PETRILLA: You scum!

GABRILLA: And you, Petrilla?

PETRILLA: Before I'd sleep with you, I'd sleep with anybody!

GABRIEL: I would satisfy your wish, nephew. This harlot doesn't matter to me and I don't need her. But she's my wife, and honor prevents me from letting her leave. I've become a powerful and respectable gentleman, and a very pious Christian. Like all rich people. Give me your arm, dear wife, and we'll go to mass and set a good example for the natives.

(*He takes her by the arm and leads her away. They both exit. PEDRO LAS CASAS follows them. Enter FRAY ANTONIO and PEDRO DE CORDOBA. The latter is ill.*)

BARTOLOME (*Going to meet them*): Fray Pedro de Córdoba! Come in and sit down.

PEDRO DE CORDOBA: My legs can still support me, in spite of my infirmities. And my voice shall not tremble when I reprimand a traitor like you. (*He coughs.*)

BARTOLOME: That word, Fray Pedro...

FRAY ANTONIO: Give him a glass of water.

PEDRO DE CORDOBA: I don't want anything of his.

FRAY ANTONIO: Rest, father.

(PEDRO DE CORDOBA sits down in a chair brought to him by PEDRO RENTERIA and MARIA, who then exit.)

PEDRO DE CORDOBA: I sent Fray Antonio with you to Spain, to present King Ferdinand with a true account of what was happening here. And a list of possible resolutions.

BARTOLOME: That is what we did.

PEDRO DE CORDOBA: You turned them inside out, making them serve your interests and greed. You had King Charles sign them so you would be granted a territory and could realize your ambition of becoming a governor.

BARTOLOME: More likely a peacemaker, Fray Pedro.

PEDRO DE CORDOBA: A commercial contract to increase the earnings of the King and the colonists.

BARTOLOME: That's not exactly true.

PEDRO DE CORDOBA: And as an even greater mockery, you are prepared to ally yourself with malefactors, corrupt captains, and bribed officials.

BARTOLOME: If you saw a crucified Christ, would you not do everything in your power to rescue him?

PEDRO DE CORDOBA: What do you mean by that question?

BARTOLOME: And if they were not willing to hand him over graciously, but they would sell him, would you not be prepared to buy him?

PEDRO DE CORDOBA: Beyond a doubt.

BARTOLOME: Well, that is what I'm trying to do. To redeem the Christ who has been treated with scorn in the Indies, I am buying him with temporal goods and income.

FRAY ANTONIO: But don't you see that they are setting a trap for you? They only want you to fail.

BARTOLOME: I will not fail.

FRAY ANTONIO: But if you did, nothing would prevent them from enslaving all of the Indians in the region.

BARTOLOME: You are forgetting Divine Providence.

FRAY ANTONIO: And you are forgetting human nature.

PEDRO DE CORDOBA: I have come to inform you that not one of our friars will accompany you on such a foolish venture.

FRAY ANTONIO: Which will only, once again, bring harm to the inhabitants of the area.

BARTOLOME: Are they not already subjected to the most crushing sorrows?

FRAY ANTONIO: You're a madman.

BARTOLOME: And you, you're far too sane.

(*PEDRO RENTERIA enters.*)

PEDRO RENTERIA: His Excellency, the Governor!
PEDRO DE CORDOBA (*Getting up, he addresses Bartolomé*): May the Lord bless you.
FRAY ANTONIO: You, and your impossible madness, Father Bartolomé.

(*The GOVERNOR enters, followed by GABRIEL, PEDRO LAS CASAS, and MARIA.*)

GABRIEL: The protocol is ready to sign.

(*The GOVERNOR sits down at the company table. The two Dominicans remain standing, downstage.*)

GOVERNOR (*Signing with solemnity*): In the name of His Majesty, King Charles I, God save the king.
GABRIEL (*Holding the document in front of Bartolomé*): Father Bartolomé...
BARTOLOME (*He approaches, takes the pen, hesitates for a few moments, and then rapidly decides*): In the name of our Lord Jesus Christ.

(*He signs quickly. There is a solemn trumpet fanfare whose music becomes distorted until it is unpleasant and almost deafening. Blackout, during which we hear as well the sounds of battle, gunshots, clashing swords, swearing, Indian war chants. Spotlight on BARTOLOME, who goes upstage and bangs on the enormous doors of the Dominican convent.*)

BARTOLOME: Hello, in the convent! Fray Antonio!

(*Suddenly there is a total silence. BARTOLOME, extremely affected and in deep sorrow, moves downstage where PETRILLA enters.*)

PETRILLA: Bartolomé, the sad news that has reached us here on the island, is it true?
BARTOLOME: Yes.
PETRILLA: My God!
BARTOLOME: We anchored our ships along the coast and solemnly proclaimed our message of peace. But there were so few of us. The soldiers who were supposed to protect us, when they realized they could not get rich, they turned back. Even so, our efforts would have been fruitful if we had not been harassed by the pearl merchants on the nearby islands who trade wine for slaves.
PETRILLA: And you?

BARTOLOME: I came to Santo Domingo to ask the Governor for relief. But in my absence the natives rebelled. I should have died with my people, among the flames, at the door of the chapel, forgiving those who only defended themselves, not knowing the difference between one group of Spaniards and another.

PETRILLA: Were there survivors?

BARTOLOME: Some managed to escape along the river. But my father died, and my friend Rentería, and his wife María, one of the gentlest souls I have ever known.

PETRILLA: And my son? They hid him in Tierras Perdidas. I wanted to go with you to be at his side.

BARTOLOME: No, Petrilla, I'm sorry. I know nothing of him.

PETRILLA: Gabriel is going to charter some ships.

BARTOLOME: No doubt on a campaign of vengeance, to punish the assault on our village.

PETRILLA: No!

BARTOLOME: Perhaps they only expected from me a pretext for killing off the territory's inhabitants. They all ridicule me now and say that the only way to deal with Indians is conquest or slavery. And that's untrue. It's a miserable lie!

PETRILLA (*Embracing him chastely*): Bartolomé...

BARTOLOME: Señor, my good, kind Señor, what have I done to you and to your people? I've killed you now a second time.

(*As Bartolomé speaks, we hear the sound of Señor's flute. Then silence. A long silence.*)

VOICE OF FRAY ANTONIO: Who's there?

PETRILLA (*In a neutral tone*): Father Bartolomé de Las Casas: priest, colonist, and Spaniard. Friend of Chancellors and Kings, administrator of the Pearl Coast, Apostle of the Indians.

BARTOLOME: An unworthy and repentant sinner, who introduced black slaves and tolerated the enslavement of rebels. Who brought ruin to his family and friends and to the Indians he claimed to protect. A ridiculous and pretentious young gentleman from Seville who was going to redeem the colonies of the New World with his arrogance. Who asks to be received by Your Order as the humblest and most inept of your friars.

(*The door has opened. PETRILLA stands to one side. FRAY ANTONIO appears.*)

FRAY ANTONIO: Bartolomé!

BARTOLOME: Antonio! Take me to Fray Pedro de Córdoba.

PEDRO DE CORDOBA (*Entering*): We expected you, brother. God be praised for bringing you and for preserving my feeble life so that I could receive you in my arms.

(*He embraces Bartolomé. Sound of bells. Escorted by FRAY ANTON and PEDRO DE CORDOBA, BARTOLOME goes upstage to enter the convent. A choir of friars chants a Te Deum and joins in a procession. Above the religious music can be heard, once again, the sound of the flute.*)

END OF THE THIRD ACT

ACT IV

Madrid, 1566, at the Convent of Santa María de Atocha. The cell of FRAY BARTOLOME DE LAS CASAS, who is now ninety years old. He was writing in front of a large window, but he has fallen asleep over his papers.

A friar enters. It is RODRIGO DE ANDRADA, carrying a bowl of soup and a jug of water. He is the same actor who played Pedro de Rentería.

FRAY RODRIGO: Bishop, Your Excellency!

BARTOLOME (*Waking up*): Not bishop. Not excellency.

FRAY RODRIGO: You have not lost your title even if you have renounced your diocese.

BARTOLOME: I am only a friar, like you. Humbler than you, for you have not failed in your endeavors as I have, over and over.

FRAY RODRIGO: Don't say that.

BARTOLOME: Although I'm smarter, that's true. I would never have chosen somebody like me as a companion.

FRAY RODRIGO: You are a blinding light that illuminates all that surrounds you.

BARTOLOME: And you are a flatterer. You know perfectly well what I'm like. A great sinner who has never learned to protect his Indians.

FRAY RODRIGO: You have dedicated your life to them.

BARTOLOME: Every injustice, every death will weigh upon my soul at the last judgment.

FRAY RODRIGO: That is not true.

BARTOLOME: At one time, I asked for black slaves, as if they, too, were not my brothers.

FRAY RODRIGO: Greatly have you repented that, Monsignor.

BARTOLOME: I accepted the power of deciding which Indians should be reduced to slavery.

FRAY RODRIGO: But you never enslaved any of them.

BARTOLOME: No one can accept that power, because no one has rights over the life of a fellow being. Even if you don't use that power. And my father and my best friends died in Tierra Firme, victims of my own failure.

FRAY RODRIGO: I've brought you some soup.

BARTOLOME: Again?

FRAY RODRIGO: Are you never hungry?

BARTOLOME: That was always my mother's desire: to make me eat. I'll have it later. Let me write, Fray Pedro.

FRAY RODRIGO: Don't call me Pedro, Monsignor. I'm Fray Rodrigo.

BARTOLOME: Well you look just like my friend Pedro Rentería.

FRAY RODRIGO: I never even met him.

BARTOLOME: I don't believe you. You and he are identical.

FRAY RODRIGO: Put on your cape. You're going to get chilled. (*He helps Bartolomé to put it on.*)

BARTOLOME: Bah!

FRAY RODRIGO: I met you the day you first put on this Dominican habit.

BARTOLOME: That was a long time ago. More than twenty years.

FRAY RODRIGO: Almost forty, Monsignor. I was still a child.

BARTOLOME: Where is Fray Pedro de Córdoba?

FRAY RODRIGO: Fray Pedro died when I was a novitiate.

BARTOLOME: He truly was that light you were speaking of a moment ago. Call Fray Antonio Montesinos.

FRAY RODRIGO: But...

BARTOLOME: That's what exasperates me about you. You never carry out my wishes promptly.

FRAY RODRIGO: Fray Antonio died in Venezuela.

BARTOLOME: That doesn't matter. Have him come. I must make confession. I cannot come to the end of my days without being absolved of my terrible sins.

FRAY RODRIGO: Fray Antonio forgave you many times.

BARTOLOME: That's not enough! Fray Antonio! Fray Antonio!

FRAY RODRIGO: In God's name, be still. You'll disturb the whole convent.

BARTOLOME: Then go to look for him at once. Fray Antonio!

FRAY RODRIGO: All right, all right... (*He humors Fray Bartolomé in order to calm him down. Exit.*)

FRAY ANTONIO (*Appearing on the upper stage*): What's all the shouting about?

BARTOLOME: Well, finally. Your calmness is as insulting as ever. Come in, don't just stand there. Close the windows. I don't want anyone to hear us. (*The upstage curtain is closed and the light changes*). It's been a while since you've seen me. Well, how do I look?

FRAY ANTONIO: The passage of time affects us all.

BARTOLOME: Not you.

FRAY ANTONIO: Memories are ageless.

BARTOLOME: I don't have a mirror, you know. So I cannot see how old my face looks. Ninety years old! I don't know anyone who's lived that long. I feel tired, Fray Antonio, very tired. And that is my great temptation. To abandon the fight and rest forever. I have called so that you may absolve me of this evil desire.

FRAY ANTONIO: I cannot do that, Bartolomé.

BARTOLOME: I gave the Indians they allocated to me back to the Governor. Nothing prevents you from doing it.

FRAY ANTONIO: You cannot receive forgiveness from a memory.

BARTOLOME: Why did you leave me alone? Alone with my letters, my papers, the denunciations I made to the King, to the Pope, to the

Chancellors. Insignificant drops of water in an infinite sea. What made you abandon me, Fray Antonio?

FRAY ANTONIO: You know very well. It was death.

BARTOLOME: They say you were poisoned. You should have been more careful! Try the soup. Eat. (*FRAY ANTONIO does so.*) How could you not notice the taste of the poison? Bitter, sour, different. You've always been a bumpkin incapable of subleties. (*FRAY ANTONIO gets up.*) Where are you going? I forbid you to leave my side. I want you present for my audience with the Emperor.

FRAY ANTONIO: I hate politics.

BARTOLOME: His royal conscience is disturbed, filled with doubts. They have just requested my presence so that I can tell him what is happening in his dominions across the sea.

FRAY ANTONIO: I was not at that interview.

BARTOLOME: Well now you can't refuse. You are under my control. That's the best part about dreams. You will remain at my side as long as I want. (*PETRILLA has entered.*) Here again, Petrilla? Don't you know that women are not allowed to enter this cloister?

PETRILLA: Even in your thoughts?

BARTOLOME: It's like a nightmare, Fray Antonio. She's constantly coming into my cell. I try to throw her out, but she always comes back.

PETRILLA: Can I drink from your jug? You shall know my secrets. Although all Seville knows who is the owner of my heart.

BARTOLOME: There must be more than one.

PETRILLA: No one like you. Not now or ever!

BARTOLOME: Let me alone.

PETRILLA: I didn't mean to offend you. On the contrary, I thought you would be happy to to know that in spite of your friar's habit, for me you're still a man.

BARTOLOME: Go away, go away. Please, Fray Antonio, tell her that I'm ninety years old and she should leave me in peace.

FRAY ANTONIO: Señora, why have you come?

PETRILLA: He's the one who keeps calling me.

BARTOLOME: Don't you believe it.

PETRILLA: He likes to remember the day his uncle died. In some ways it was his triumph, his only triumph, in the Indies. You know how vain he is.

BARTOLOME: You are a devil, Petrilla.

PETRILLA: Gabriel was very ill. I told him so that day. And he responded, irritated.

BARTOLOME: What does that matter to me.

PETRILLA: He wants to see you, I added.

BARTOLOME: Well I don't want anything to do with him. Let him croak.

FRAY ANTONIO: You shouldn't say that, Fray Bartolomé.

BARTOLOME: He was always a tyrant, the scourge of my poor Indians.

PETRILLA: Yesterday they gave him the last rites.

BARTOLOME: A sacrilege. No one can forgive him unless he first returns what does not belong to him.

PETRILLA: To me, that son of a bitch doesn't mean a thing! But he's yelling for you like someone possessed by the devil.

FRAY ANTONIO: Are you going to refuse?

BARTOLOME: Let him die with his riches, his mines, and his slave ships!

FRAY ANTONIO: Without hearing him?

BARTOLOME: Oh, aren't you going to leave me in peace even in my dreams! Always the same scene, the same words. I can't get it out of my mind!

(*FRAY ANTONIO has brought GABRIEL in his wheelchair.*)

GABRIEL: You almost didn't make it on time. And it would have been a real pity, because I'm going to give you a magnificent farewell present.

BARTOLOME: I shall accept nothing from you, uncle.

GABRIEL: Wait until you find out what it is. Petrilla, bring me pen and paper and a notary to take down my last will and testament word for word. (*She gives them to Fray Antonio, who writes.*) "I, Gabriel, as I give up my soul to the Lord, hereby attest to my life of greed and my cruelty to the natives."

BARTOLOME: It's about time!

GABRIEL: Be quiet and listen. You're too damned impatient! "And I affirm that my nephew, Bartolomé de Las Casas, whom I love even though he has angered me ever since he stole from me the best-looking girls in Seville, including Petrilla..." (*To Fray Antonio.*) Scratch that last part, notary. "Well, I repeat and affirm that he is the only decent person in this cursed land of the devil. And he even may be right when he says that we should not force Christianity on the savages." I swear to hell!

PETRILLA: Don't get excited.

GABRIEL: I'll do as I please, witch.

PETRILLA: Well, dictate more slowly. The notary can't keep up with you.

GABRIEL: Can you hear me, nephew? That's all that matters to me.

BARTOLOME: What matters is the Indians.

GABRIEL: Bah! Savage dogs that deserve what they get.

BARTOLOME: I won't tolerate...!

GABRIEL: They killed your father and many good Christians. And they knifed each other for a miserable barrel of wine. But let's forget that. And now, notary, make sure that what I'm about to dictate is perfectly clear: "All of my property and my Indians, all of them, I leave to my nephew Bartolomé, so that he can give them back their freedom, make restitution to those who have been harmed, and undo the damage that I have done so that I may be received up there with honor." If there is anything up there.

PETRILLA: Have you lost your mind? What about me? Your wife?
GABRIEL: If nothing belongs to me, as your wonderful Bartolomé says, then nothing is yours either. So you're out on the street, without a cent. Like a beggar.
PETRILLA: All my life working and suffering for you... Isn't that worth some reward?
GABRIEL: I paid you at the time for what you are: a slut.
PETRILLA: But what can you be thinking? That you can trample on those around you, suck their last drop of blood, and then die like a saint. I'll see that you are condemned, as you deserve, and that you burn forever for being a rogue and scoundrel.
GABRIEL: Wouldn't you like that!
PETRILLA: I'll go before the Governor and the Court of Appeals. You cannot renounce your property. Your wife has rights.
GABRIEL: You'll sign your agreement to my will. I order you to do it.
PETRILLA: You're dying, Gabriel. I'm not afraid of you anymore.

(*A solemn trumpet fanfare. Enter TWO CHANCELLORS, played by the same actors as Fonseca and Conchillos. One speaks with a noticeable Flemish accent and the other with an Italian accent.*)

FIRST CHANCELLOR: His Majesty, the Emperor Charles V!
SECOND CHANCELLOR: The First of Spain!
GABRIEL: Let him wait!
PETRILLA: The Emperor?
GABRIEL: Nothing is more urgent nor more worthy of respect than His Majesty, the Grim Reaper--not even the Emperor.
PETRILLA (*Curtsying to the chancellors, who remain on stage*): It will only be a moment, Excellencies. He's about ready to give up his soul.
GABRIEL: In this life, I've bought everything. Tell me, why shouldn't I buy my salvation? After all, what do I have to lose? At any rate, I have no one to leave it to. I have no sons. Apparently my sperm is like wet powder that never explodes.
BARTOLOME: You had one.
GABRIEL: Don't lie to me, Bartolomé, not you. We both know that the son was not mine but from one of those redskins that rolled in the sack with Petrilla. Nor do I believe that he died. They must have hidden him for fear of my anger. (*To Fray Antonio.*) What are you writing? Give me that last page. (*He tears it up.*) And now, Fray Antonio, give me the last rites again, with a lot of oil so that my salvation doesn't squeak. I also have a present for you, Petrilla. At last, I'm leaving you alone. I hope that son of a bitch at least knows how to take care of his mother. The pen. (*He signs the document.*) Close it with lots of seals so there's no doubt. And hurry, Fray Antonio, or it may be too late.

(FRAY ANTONIO takes a cross and absolves him, then gives him extreme unction.)

BARTOLOME: And you, Petrilla, are you going to accept his last wishes?
PETRILLA: He's a miserable... I'll be singing and dancing from happiness at his wake.

(FRAY ANTONIO moves away from Gabriel, who has died.)

FIRST CHANCELLOR: His Majesty...
SECOND CHANCELLOR: The Emperor...
PETRILLA *(After a certain hesitation)*: Give me the document. But I'm not doing it for that miserable wretch! *(She signs it, throws the pen on the floor, and exits crying.)*

(CHARLES V enters. The EMPEROR is played by the same actor who portrayed King Ferdinand the Catholic. Solemn trumpets.)

EMPEROR: Where is that friar, who has assailed me with letters and documents throughout my reign?
BARTOLOME: Your Majesty.
EMPEROR: You must have calluses on your fingers from wielding the pen so much, and your blood has probably turned the color of ink.
BARTOLOME: My blood, Señor, is black like the iniquity I have witnessed in the Indies, and my calluses are due to my struggle for Your Majesty's justice.

(The CHANCELLORS bring a chair so the EMPEROR may sit down.)

FRAY ANTONIO: A wonderful response. My congratulations.
BARTOLOME: Well, maybe it wasn't so well turned...but after thinking about it over time, I've improved it.
FRAY ANTONIO: They're the same councilors King Ferdinand had!
BARTOLOME: You're mistaken. One of these is Flemish and the other is Italian. But ambitious men resemble one another like drops of water.
EMPEROR: I like you, Fray Bartolomé. You have a noble cause and you're admirably tenacious in defending it. Although your colonization of the Coast that I authorized years ago was a real disaster.
BARTOLOME: That can be attributed to various reasons.
EMPEROR: Water over the dam. I'm going to speak to you candidly. The matter of the Indies disturbs me a great deal. On the one hand, the Court's expenses are so high that we have to squeeze out the maximum income. On the other hand, I don't want to harm the natives. It's like squaring the circle: an impossibility.

BARTOLOME: And in the center of that circle, my Lord, is your conscience. As a King, and as a man.

EMPEROR: You're right. And you have no idea how much that blessed conscience torments me. I'm constantly asking myself if those territories really belong to us just because we conquered them.

FIRST CHANCELLOR: You must reject such scruples, Your Majesty.

SECOND CHANCELLOR: There is no greater good for those people than the true faith.

EMPEROR: You've heard the Chancellors and Theologians. But I called you because I want to know your opinion.

BARTOLOME: You're not going to like it.

EMPEROR: I'm listening.

BARTOLOME: All my life I believed that God was the King of the world and that the Pope should divide that power among the sovereigns. I now know that God does not wish that. The only sovereign is man. Whatever his color and whatever his condition.

EMPEROR: Go on.

BARTOLOME: The Indian kingdoms and communities therefore, in justice, are their own lords, and free. The least of their chieftains has the same rights and duties as the Spanish Crown or any other independent state.

SECOND CHANCELLOR: Are you forgetting the sacred message of our Religion?

BARTOLOME: As my father once advised me: never take advantage of God for your own benefit.

FIRST CHANCELLOR: That's an insult!

BARTOLOME: Their rights, human rights, are above all else.

EMPEROR: Including the Crown? Including the faith?

BARTOLOME: Including the Crown. Including the faith, Emperor!

(*Pause.*)

EMPEROR: I think you've gone too far. Although I'll tell you confidentially that on more than one occasion I've been tempted to restore those territories to their former owners in order to bring peace to my soul.

FIRST CHANCELLOR: That would be a catastrophe, Your Majesty.

SECOND CHANCELLOR: They'd go back to being pagans and idol-worshippers.

(*Short pause.*)

EMPEROR: Too far...you see. Where even the most powerful Emperor in the world cannot go. I'm going to name you to a high post. I need men like you at my side.

FIRST CHANCELLOR (*In a low voice to the Emperor*): The Court will say that you're letting yourself be influenced by a hot-headed friar who denies the Pope's authority.

SECOND CHANCELLOR (*In the same fashion*): If he sticks his nose in the Royal Treasury, the budget will be in trouble.

EMPEROR (*In a low voice to his advisers*): Do you think so?

FIRST CHANCELLOR (*The same*): Perhaps he could be made a bishop.

SECOND CHANCELLOR (*The same*): After all, he is a friar.

EMPEROR (*Speaking aloud*): Fray Bartolomé, I shall have you made a bishop.

BARTOLOME: I don't want to be a bishop!

EMPEROR: Do you dare to contradict me?

BARTOLOME: With all due respect, Your Majesty, I do not wish to renounce my life in the convent.

EMPEROR: Bishop!

BARTOLOME: Bishop, Your Majesty.

EMPEROR: We'll look for a vacant see.

FIRST CHANCELLOR: In Chiapas.

EMPEROR: Where's that?

FIRST CHANCELLOR: In the New World.

SECOND CHANCELLOR: It's only a two or three month voyage from here.

FRAY ANTONIO (*To Bartolomé*): Don't accept. They're only trying to silence your voice.

BARTOLOME: Why don't you come with me?

FRAY ANTONIO: I am to go to Mexico, to Puerto Rico, and then to Venezuela. The Emperor has leased a strip of land to some bankers from Augsburg who are far crueler than any Spaniard.

BARTOLOME (*To the Emperor*): You've turned your dominion over to a foreigner?

EMPEROR: I couldn't find other moneylenders willing to advance me any funds.

BARTOLOME (*To Fray Antonio*): Those Germans will have you poisoned.

FRAY ANTONIO: What difference does it make if you die one way or another. What matters is how you live.

EMPEROR: The time is up. Give to each of them what he has coming according to my justice.

FIRST CHANCELLOR (*To Bartolomé*): For you, a miter. (*He puts it on Bartolomé's head.*)

SECOND CHANCELLOR (*To Fray Antonio*): And for you, your nightly soup in the convent dining hall.

BARTOLOME (*To Fray Antonio*): You have him here, right now. Ask the Emperor whatever you want before he goes away forever. Denounce those Germans who are going to poison you.

FRAY ANTONIO: Your Majesty...I...

BARTOLOME: Go ahead.

FRAY ANTONIO: Do not forget your subjects, especially the unfortunate ones.

FIRST CHANCELLOR (*Solemnly*): Make way for the Emperor!

(*The EMPEROR and his CHANCELLORS exit. Perhaps we hear the trumpets again. Then the sound of thuds.*)

FRAY ANTONIO: What's that?

BARTOLOME: Stones. Against the cathedral door in my diocese. Everyone is angry at me. Even the priests. Even the victims have sided with their oppressors.

FRAY ANTONIO: Corruption is contagious because everyone hopes to get a share of it.

BARTOLOME: That's why I renounced my bishopric and returned to Spain. To write. That's all I can do now.

FRAY ANTONIO: As for me, they buried me in a common grave.

BARTOLOME: But no one will ever forget your Advent sermon.

FRAY ANTONIO: Fray Pedro de Córdoba dictated it to me. I simply transmitted it to my parishioners.

BARTOLOME: Rest easy. My writings speak of you.

FRAY ANTONIO: And what will be the fate of your writings?

BARTOLOME: They say that it's my fault that there will be a legend discrediting our country. Apparently the deeds themselves do not matter! What they won't tolerate is someone denouncing them.

FRAY ANTONIO: They will say of you that you hated your fellow countrymen.

BARTOLOME: That's not true! You and I, we are just as much Spanish as the conquistadors or the slave hunters although we do not agree with their methods. Spain is great not just because of her victories and her heroes but because she has had sons like you, Fray Antonio de Montesinos. I confess that I do admire your humility, your honesty, that integrity of a poor friar from Extremadura.

FRAY ANTONIO: And I do admire your tireless obstinancy...of a gentleman from Andalusia.

(*They embrace with deep emotion. Enter FRAY RODRIGO DE ANDRADA.*)

FRAY RODRIGO: Have you calmed down, Monsignor? What are you doing in the dark? (*He draws open the curtains. Real light from the window. FRAY ANTONIO exits.*) The mail has arrived with your correspondence. (*He hands Fray Bartolomé a pile of papers and scrolls.*) They come from everywhere, from Europe and from the New World.

BARTOLOME: Anything from Rome?

FRAY RODRIGO: It's too early to have a response from the Pope.

BARTOLOME: You see. Not even the Pope is moved. Get that miter out of my sight.

FRAY RODRIGO: You have a visitor, Monsignor.

BARTOLOME: I don't want to receive anyone.

FRAY RODRIGO: He's come from very far just to see you.

BARTOLOME: It must be one of those pretentious courtiers. (*He sits down to open his correspondence.*) What do you want now?

FRAY RODRIGO: He doesn't look like someone from the Court. He's an Indian. At least he has dark skin.

BARTOLOME: An Indian here, in Atocha?

FRAY RODRIGO: He calls himself Señor.

BARTOLOME: Señor?

FRAY RODRIGO: Yes. That's what I think...

BARTOLOME: It's impossible. Have him come in immediately.

FRAY RODRIGO: Yes, Your Excellency.

(*FRAY RODRIGO has SEÑOR enter. He is about fifty years old. His hair is partially gray. He has a noble bearing and speaks softly but firmly. He is dressed like a Spaniard and is played by the same actor who portrayed his namesake, the Indian boy.*)

BARTOLOME (*Very troubled*): Señor! I've expected you for so many years. I didn't think I'd ever find you again. Let me kiss your feet. (*He is about to kneel, as Señor did at the beginning of the play.*)

SEÑOR: Your Excellency, for me? What are you doing? (*He prevents Bartolomé from kneeling.*)

BARTOLOME: I can barely remember how you look. Your hair is gray now, and your face is lined with wrinkles. But, thank God, no one can turn off the luster in your eyes.

SEÑOR: This is the first time you've seen me, Monsignor.

BARTOLOME: Don't say that.

SEÑOR: Although I have had you in my thoughts since I reached the age of reason. My mother spoke so much about Your Excellency.

BARTOLOME: Your mother? Who are you?

SEÑOR: Señor.

BARTOLOME: You're lying. You are not Señor. He would never have called me Excellency as you have just done.

SEÑOR: I am Petrilla's son, and my name is Señor.

BARTOLOME: Excuse me. She gave you that name in memory of another Señor whom we knew a long time ago.

SEÑOR: She told me about him.

BARTOLOME: Come in. Sit down.

SEÑOR (*Bending over Bartolomé's hands, he kisses them*): I have waited for this moment so long, Excellency.

BARTOLOME: Petrilla...a great woman.

SEÑOR: She tells many stories of the days when you went to the tavern where she worked. Lies, no doubt!

BARTOLOME: Or truths. After so many years, it's almost the same.

SEÑOR: I know all the names, of your father, your uncle Gabriel, of Pedro Rentería, and María, and so many others.

BARTOLOME: It was a world of adventurers and ambitious men, of heroes and riffraff. No worse than today's world, unfortunately. Only your mother and I are left from that other one.

SEÑOR: She got for me, only the Lord knows through what sacrifices, enough money to pay my passage to Spain so I could see you.

BARTOLOME: Your mother could have been rich, but she signed the paper renouncing the wealth her husband had adquired through unjust means.

SEÑOR: I know. I also feel proud of my father, whoever he was. I am not the son of this one or that one, like everyone else, but of a whole race.

BARTOLOME: Do you know how to play the flute?

SEÑOR: No, Monsignor.

BARTOLOME: Pity. I would have liked to hear it one more time, before I die.

SEÑOR: I'm a poet. The Indian who hid me taught be all that he could. I have compiled the elegies and poems of a vanquished people, some of them from before colonization. That, too, was a cruel world, with slaves and wars and sacrifices on the altars of the gods.

BARTOLOME: We were supposed to show them the good, not change one cruelty for another.

SEÑOR: Sometimes I think that the New World will not be either yours, Excellency, or my father's. His was only the land of that land. We shall be the New World, we mestizos. We shall create a new race of free people, with their own banner and their own king, without chains to bind them to the ancient rites or to the foreign sovereigns from across the sea.

BARTOLOME: Be quiet. Even to think it is a crime.

SEÑOR: And that day we shall light bonfires on the tops of the mountains, we shall dress in white, and adorn ourselves with crowns of flowers. We shall eat all the goat meat we want and it will rain, it will rain for thirty days to make our fields fertile.

BARTOLOME: They can hear us.

SEÑOR: And do you know what we shall do that day? We'll raise a great monument to those like you, to honor the best that we received from your country: your faith, your language, and your heart.

BARTOLOME: Those are only the fantasies of a poet.

SEÑOR: The blood that runs through half my veins is that of Spaniards like you, not of those who martyred the other half of my body with their gunpowder, their dogs, and their irons.

BARTOLOME: I always said that my country would be punished for their sins.

SEÑOR: And redeemed by its virtues. According to the Scriptures, a single just man can save an entire city.

BARTOLOME (*Referring to some papers that Señor holds in his right hand*): Are those your poems?

SEÑOR: I brought them for you. (*He hands them over.*) They tell the tragedy of the vanquished.

FRAY RODRIGO (*Entering*): Excellency...

BARTOLOME (*Leafing through them*): Dedicated, I see, to the ancient gods.

SEÑOR: They, too, were vanquished, Monsignor.

FRAY RODRIGO: The community is assembled in the chapel for prayer, like every evening.

BARTOLOME: To Tonantzin, the goddess of life and fertility.

SEÑOR: Through her miracle I was kept alive when I was born.

BARTOLOME: You're not Christian?

SEÑOR: Oh, yes, Monsignor.

BARTOLOME: And pagan?

SEÑOR: That too. A little. Like all of us.

FRAY RODRIGO: It's time, Monsignor...

BARTOLOME: Be quiet! (*To Señor.*) I want to give you something. (*He takes off the medal of the Zailos that he wears hanging from his neck.*) It was given to me by someone whose name was the same as yours. Perhaps you also have blood from his tribe. Hang it from your neck and wear it always.

FRAY RODRIGO: Your candle, Excellency.

BARTOLOME (*Shoving it away*): I don't have time left to pray. I still have to write so many letters, so many grievances, so many petitions.

FRAY RODRIGO: Later, Excellency.

BARTOLOME: You help me, Señor. My hand shakes when I pick up the pen. Write. Quickly. Excommunication for those who declare war against the Indians. Bishops should learn the languages of their parishioners. Restitution of gold, pearls, and precious stones. Don't stop! Let dignity be restored to the native lords. (*He has been talking faster and faster and almost cannot be understood. He stops to catch his breath.*)

FRAY RODRIGO (*Handing him the lighted candle*): Here. They're waiting for you.

BARTOLOME (*To Señor*): Come with me to the choir. Later you can transcribe while I dictate. Ninety years old and I have achieved nothing of what I intended. Nothing!

SEÑOR: My brothers worship you. And you have disciples and followers in Spain and throughout the earth.

BARTOLOME: But that world is so large, dear Lord, so large. There are so many paths to follow, so many seas to cross. (*At the back of the stage, transparent as if it were the chapel window, is an enormous, old map of the Americas. Dominican friars, bearing lighted candles, enter from each side. They have their hoods covering their faces. Sound of gregorian music. A shot rings out and there is light on the upper stage. The deck of a ship. PEDRO LAS CASAS is standing there.*)

PEDRO LAS CASAS: It's the cannon on the captain's ship. They've raised the banner to the Virgin Mary!

SEÑOR: In Chile, in Mexico, in Venezuela, Panama, Puerto Rico, Cuba, Santo Domingo and Guatemala. Antigua, Trinidad, Peru, Ecuador, Colombia... Florida, California. (*White lights appear at each spot on the map as it is named.*)

PEDRO LAS CASAS: My son, may this land give you the honor and glory that you seek.

BARTOLOME: I ask God's forgiveness for having done so little for my fellow human beings across the sea. And to you, my friars, I ask you from my knees that you help me to atone for this sin. (*He kneels.*)

PEDRO LAS CASAS: You are a learned man and a teacher of Church doctrine.

BARTOLOME: All that I have said and written throughout my life is based on truth and even so I have fallen short of describing the causes that have moved me to my endeavors. (*The friars begin to remove their hoods. They are the characters from the play.*) What are you doing here, Mother? And you, Petrilla? Don't you know that it's forbidden? Governor, Your Honor! Uncle Gabriel! María! Fray Pedro! And you, Fray Antonio Montesinos, give me your hand! Swear to me before God, all of you, that you will never abandon my Indians. They are like orphans. Protect them, protect them...

(*FRAY RODRIGO has taken the candle from him. SEÑOR puts it out and crosses himself. BARTOLOME falls face down on the floor.*)

PEDRO LAS CASAS: May the Lord bless you, Bartolomé.

FRAY ANTONIO: One year after his death, his adversaries declared the freedom of the Indians of Cobán, in Guatemala, whom he had converted. That was the first of many battles to be won after his death by Fray Bartolomé de Las Casas, utopian dreamer and hyperbolic visionary, but the Great Apostle and Defender of the Indies.

(*They have all withdrawn. BARTOLOME remains alone, on the floor, in the spotlight. The map has become dark and the lights of the cities are like stars in a clear sky watching over his body. A long pause.*)

THE END

Photo: Juan José Sánchez
Jaime Salom's *Bonfire at Dawn*, Mexico, 1990

CRITICAL REACTION TO THE MEXICAN PRODUCTION

"Successful opening for Bartolomé de Las Casas play, *Bonfire at Dawn*"

....How important and interesting it is to know, understand, and reflect upon the life of Fray Bartolomé de Las Casas, Defender of the Indians. During much of his life he fought so that those innocent people would have their liberty and cease to be treated like slaves.

The play has left a mark on everyone who saw it and who responded with deep emotion to a man who gave himself to his cause, to a priest who, tired from his struggle, reached the end of his life without knowing that a year later his objective would be realized: the Indians would receive their freedom.

Luz Elena Chavez G.
Excelsior, 2 September 1990

"Resounding success of *Bartolomé de Las Casas*"

The interesting aspect of his [Salom's] text is its historical truthfulness and the way he has structured his characters, who reflect for us the brutality of the conquistadors when they arrived in the New World.

We believe that Salom's story will not serve the goals of the organizers of the so-called "encounter of two cultures." Basing himself on history, the Spanish playwright has woven his fiction in order to make his text solidly theatrical. He offers us a wrenching, humiliating, and powerful vision of those who call themselves the founders of this Mestizo America.

Guadalupe Pereyra
El Nacional, 2 September 1990

ABOUT THE TRANSLATOR

Phyllis Zatlin is Professor of Spanish and director of translator training in the Department of Spanish and Portuguese of Rutgers, The State University of New Jersey. A specialist in contemporary theatre, she has published numerous books, editions, and articles, including a Twayne World Authors Series volume on Jaime Salom. Her translations of contemporary Spanish short stories have appeared in *Short Story International*, *Kansas Quarterly*, and *Crab Creek Review*. Stagings of her translations of plays by Paloma Pedrero and José Luis Alonso de Santos are scheduled for 1991-92 at Pace University (New York City) and University of Missouri (Kansas City).

TRANSLATOR'S ACKNOWLEDGEMENTS

I should like to express my appreciation to Martha T. Halsey, whose enthusiasm and tireless efforts made this new translation series possible; to Marion P. Holt, for sharing his considerable knowledge of translating plays for publication and performance; to Roger Cornish, Manuel Duque, and Felicia Hardison Londré, for their helpful suggestions on the translation in progress; to Carol Reilly, for her conscientious attention to the final manuscript; and to The Pennsylvania State University, The Program for Cultural Cooperation Between Spain's Ministry of Culture and the United States Universities, and the Cultural Office of the Spanish Embassy in Washington for their support of this project. Above all, my continuing gratitude to Jaime Salom for his friendship over the years, as well as for his full cooperation in the preparation of this translation. The slight changes I made to the original text of *Una hoguera en el amanecer* in creating a version for American audiences were done with his knowledge and approval.

P. Z.

Las Casas: Una hoguera en el amanecer ("Bonfire at Dawn")

When I was a young boy in Argentina, I read books describing Colón's conquest of the New World. I remember that those books were full of engravings showing beautifully dressed men -- strong, valient, audacious men -- decked out in jewelry and carrying shiny swords. I admired them and associated them with the buccaneers or the "Clark Kent/Superman" of my time. Those were real adventure books, the books of my childhood.

But I also remember the Indians in those engravings. Their physical attitude was one of adoration, of offering their riches, their values and their beliefs to a superior, almost magical God. Through the eyes of the Spanish artists of the early explorations, these Indians seem open and candid as they approach their new conquerors.

In my early school years I didn't think about the tragedy that resulted from that encounter, or how painful the passage must have been from freedom and admiration to slavery, exploitation and destruction. I remember seeing, in the same books, pictures of the Jesuits -- priests with their arms extended out towards the Indians, their faces benevolent, almost sad. Although not as exciting to me as the brave conquistadors, these priests struck me as different kinds of heroes, like mother-figures who want to do the best for you without really knowing how, yet they do it anyway.

With time I learned the more or less "real" history of the Spanish Conquest. I realized that it was the priests who came to America shortly after the discovery who helped promote the exchange of language, ideas and customs, resulting in the merging of several cultures. Eventually, as history tells us, the native population revolted against the Spanish Crown, achieved independence, and suffered (as it continues to suffer) other intrusions. But their sense of identity and self-respect was something deeply understood by those humble and tenacious priests, who were crazy enough to leave the peace and comfort of their convents in Europe to adventure into an unknown world and fight for justice in the midst of the chaotic conquest.

When I first read *Las Casas: Una hoguera al amanecer*, I was impressed by the way Fray Bartolomé was portrayed. Unlike the sanctified Catholic figures I remembered from my school books, this Fray Bartolomé is brought to life as a human being, full of emotions and conflicts and totally connected to this political, social world. Here, Fray Bartolomé is an important element in the everyday fights and political maneuverings that characterized the Spanish enterprise. Above all, the play reveals his great passion for and commitment to the New World. All of the characters in *Las Casas* are alive; they have reason to interact dramatically, as opposed to simply being historical characters who are pulled together for didactic purposes. The relationship between Fray Bartolomé and Fray Antonio Montesinos is a profound statement about the clash between capitalistic and spiritual beliefs; between the dictates of the State and those of the Soul.

As described by playwright Jaime Salom, Fray Bartolomé is the quintessential man of our times, a modern hero. Confronted with the power and wealth of a virgin land, this man finds the strength to fight not only his own internal battle, but also to strike out against the abuse of the native labor force by the colonizers, the hierarchy of the Catholic Church, and the atrocities occuring in Spain. Fray Bartolomé is truly the first defender of the human rights of indigenous peoples.

To direct *Las Casas* is for me a kind of catharsis, a "fait accompli" of my own vision of the Spanish-American saga. Ultimately, it is an attempt to rescue an important lesson from the pitiful and stirring historical events of the fifteenth century; a plea to recognize the humanity in all of us and to strengthen our commitment to preserving justice in our uniquely "New World" society.

Hugo Medrano
Producing/Artistic Director
GALA Hispanic Theater
Washington, D.C.

ESTRENO: CONTEMPORARY SPANISH PLAYS SERIES

General Editor: Martha Halsey

No. 1   Jaime Salom: BONFIRE AT DAWN
         Translated by Phyllis Zatlin

No. 2   José López Rubio: IN AUGUST WE PLAY THE
         PYRENNES
         Translated by Marion P. Holt

No. 3   Ramón del Vale-Inclán: SAVAGE ACTS: FOUR
         ONE-ACT PLAYS
         Translated by Robert Lima

   A continuing series representing Spanish plays of
several generations and varying theatrical approaches
selected for their potential interest to American audiences.
Published every 9-12 months.
   Forthcoming plays will include works of Buero-Vallejo,
Antonio Gala, Paloma Pedrero and others.

   Subscriptions: Standing orders for the series or orders
for individual plays should be sent to:

ESTRENO
350 N. Burrowes Bldg.
University Park, PA 16802
U. S. A.

$6.00 per play including postage.

ESTRENO: CUADERNOS DEL TEATRO ESPAÑOL
CONTEMPORANEO

Founded in 1975 at the University of Cincinnati by Patricia
O'Connor

Editor: Martha Halsey
Assoc. Editor: Phyllis Zatlin
Book Review Editor: Wilma Newbury
Editorial Coordinator: Olga Gallego

A journal featuring play texts of previously unpublished
works from contemporary Spain, interviews with
playwrights, directors, and critics, and extensive
critical studies in both Spanish and English.

Plays published have included texts by Buero-Vallejo,
Sastre, Arrabal, Gala, Nieva, Salom, Martín Recuerda,
Olmo, Martínez Mediero, F. Cabal, P. Pedrero and Onetti.
The journal carries numerous photographs of recent
play performances in Spain and elsewhere, including
performances in translation.

Also featured are an annual bibliography, regular book
reviews, and critiques of the recent theater season, as
well as a round table in which readers from both the U. S.
and Spain share information and engage in lively debates.

ESTRENO also publishes a series of translations of
contemporary Spanish plays which may be subscribed to
separately.

Subscriptions: Orders should be sent to

ESTRENO
350 N. Burrowes Bldg.
University Park, PA 16802
U. S. A.

Individual subscriptions are $14.00 and institutional
subscriptions, $23.00 for the calendar year.

PLAYS OF THE NEW DEMOCRATIC SPAIN (1975-1990)

Contents

Hardback .... 57.58 (+ tax)
Paperback .... 32.50 (+ tax)*
* Special discount for Estreno readers:
Paperback 28.00

Orders:

Estreno
Department of Romance Languages (ML 377)
University of Cincinnati
Cincinnati, OH 45221
U. S. A.